VOICES
in the
FAMILY

VOICES
in the
FAMILY

A Therapist Talks About
Listening, Openness,
And Healing

DANIEL GOTTLIEB, PhD

Sterling Publishing Co., Inc.
New York

Grateful acknowledgment is made for the right to reprint excerpts from the following:
The Good Apprentice by Iris Murdoch, Viking, 1985
We: Understanding the Psychology of Romantic Love by Robert A. Johnson, Harper &
Row, 1985
"The Mother Journey," by Molly Layton from *The Family Therapy Networker* magazine,
September/October 1989, © 1989 by The Family Therapy Network, Inc. Reprinted by
permission of the author.
"Study War No More—Sons Forgive Fathers," by Franklin Abbott, in Voices: *The Art
and Science of Psychotherapy*, vol. 23, no. 3, Fall 1987

Library of Congress Cataloging-in-Publication Data

Gottlieb, Daniel, 1946-
  Voices in the family : a therapist talks about listening,
openness, and healing / Daniel Gottlieb.
      p. cm.
  Rev. ed. of: Family matters. 1991.
  ISBN-10: 1-4027-4760-8
  ISBN-13: 978-1-4027-4760-1
  1. Family psychotherapy--Popular works. 2. Family--Psychological aspects--Popular
works. 3. Love. I. Gottlieb, Daniel, 1946-. Family matters. II. Title.

RC488.5.G67 2007
616.89'156--dc22
                                        2007002083

2   4   6   8   10   9   7   5   3   1

Published by Sterling Publishing Co., Inc.
387 Park Avenue South, New York, NY 10016
Copyright © 2007 by Daniel Gottlieb
Previously published in 1991 by Signet and by Dutton under the title *Family Matters*.
Distributed in Canada by Sterling Publishing
c/o Canadian Manda Group, 165 Dufferin Street
Toronto, Ontario, Canada M6K 3H6
Distributed in the United Kingdom by GMC Distribution Services
Castle Place, 166 High Street, Lewes, East Sussex, England BN7 1XU
Distributed in Australia by Capricorn Link (Australia) Pty. Ltd.
P.O. Box 704, Windsor, NSW 2756, Australia

Printed in China
All rights reserved

Sterling ISBN-13: 978-1-4027-4760-1
        ISBN-10: 1-4027-4760-8

For information about custom editions, special sales, premium and
corporate purchases, please contact Sterling Special Sales
Department at 800-805-5489 or specialsales@sterlingpub.com.

Designed by Susan Fazekas

Several months after the accident that severed my spinal cord, I was at Magee Rehabilitation Center in Philadelphia. I was terribly depressed about my accident and what life would be like for a quadriplegic. I went into the cafeteria one day and saw a man of about seventy who was blind as a result of diabetes and had just had his second leg amputated. He was flirting and laughing with the nurse who was feeding him. I was struck by what spirit he had—how he, in the face of tragedy and death, was able to find joy.

I therefore would like to dedicate this book to my sightless, legless, joyful brother at Magee—to his human spirit and the human spirit in all of us.

—Daniel Gottlieb, PhD

A Note on This Edition

The idea for this book was born in the late 1980s during a Friday-night poker game with some of the teaching faculty at the Family Institute of Philadelphia. I remember complaining to Jeff Marks, a good friend as well as a poker companion, that I had a book inside of me that needed to come out, but I didn't know what it was about. His comment was: "Why don't you write about *Family Matters?*"

At that time, *Family Matters* was the title of the radio show that I hosted on WHYY, the PBS radio station in Philadelphia. With Jeff's comment, I saw at once how the contents of that show—including the responses of hundreds of listeners—could become the heart of the book that I wanted to write. So for helping to give birth to that, my first book, I would like to thank Jeff.

In the nearly twenty years since then, I have continued to host the weekly radio show on WHYY—though its name has been changed from *Family Matters* to *Voices in the Family.* I have also been writing a bimonthly column for the *Philadelphia Inquirer,* and have published two other books. In some ways, my views of myself and the world have changed. But this book, *Voices in the Family,* remains the core expression of what I wish to say about our parents, our mates, our children, ourselves—as well as my fundamental beliefs about the roles that each of us plays in the lives of others. I am grateful to see it in print again.

Contents

Introduction **1**

Part One: Our Parents **10**

1. Listening to Our Parents **11**
2. Understanding Our Relationship with Our Parents **17**
3. What Happens When Our Parents Have Crises? **28**
4. Coping with a Parent's Addiction **35**
5. How Can They Let Go of Us—
   and How Can We Let Go of Them? **47**
6. How Can We Feel Safe with Them? **54**
7. How Can We Make It Safe *for* Them? **61**
8. What Do We Expect of Our Parents? **65**
9. Learning Our Parents' Losses **72**
10. Making Peace with Our Parents **78**

Part Two: Our Mates **83**

11. Falling in Love—the Great Hallucination **84**
12. Our Fantasy of the Marriage **95**
13. Secrets Kept, Secrets Shared **103**
14. Sexual Issues: Living with Change **108**
15. From Johnandmary to John and Mary **114**
16. Power Struggles: What Does *He* Want?
    What Does *She* Want? **120**
17. The Impact of Children **128**
18. When Divorce Seems the Answer **135**
19. As a Marriage Matures **144**
20. Making Peace with Our Mates **149**

Part Three: Our Children 155

21. Listening to Our Children **156**

22. What Do We Expect of Our Children? **168**

23. Children and Anger **174**

24. Secrets Between Parent and Child **185**

25. Do Our Children Feel Safe with Us? **192**

26. Children's Sexuality—What It Means to Us **199**

27. The Impact of Divorce **209**

28. When Our Children Grow Up **217**

29. Making Peace with Our Children **224**

Part Four: Our Selves 229

30. Our Place in the Family, Our Place in the World **230**

31. What Do We Do with Anger? **239**

32. When We Feel Guilt **245**

33. When We Feel Shame **252**

34. Achievement: Is It Ever Enough? **258**

35. How Do We Live with Our Secret Selves? **264**

36. When Are We Trying to Change Our Selves? **270**

37. When We Think About Death **276**

38. Making Peace with Our Selves **281**

Conclusion: A Note on Healing **287**

Acknowledgments **294**

Introduction

In writing this book, I grappled not only with what it means to be human but also with the problem of how to describe our humanness.

The trouble, of course, is that there is so much variety to what we feel and who we are—that our lives are shaped by experiences with our families, our loved ones, our children, and our selves. Generalizations are helpful, but they are never entirely true. Examples can be misleading. We can describe certain feelings, but they are so intermingled, and the mix inside us is so extraordinary, that those feelings can never be perfectly captured. Language is always inadequate.

All the time I was writing this book, I worried about the words. Part of that came naturally: I have always worried about the way things are said and the messages people hear. The assumptions that we make about other people are implied in our words. So, too, are the expectations that we have, the ways of imposing our views on others and of expressing our own views of life. Often the words that we mean to be loving are used to control others, to convince them—and, of course, to convey what is going on inside ourselves. And since words are so important in our human relationships, they are essential to understanding our humanness.

But which words—which language—shall we use with each other?

In my writing, I have intentionally avoided, as much as possible, the language of psychological theory. That's neither my language nor the language of my therapy, and I knew from the outset it would not be the language of this book. You will find few theoretical terms, and no reports on studies of the family or statistics on human behavior. The reason is plain: That language may be fine for understanding and analysis, and it is certainly well suited for interoffice communication among professionals, but as a language of feeling, it is practically useless.

The language that I use in this book is the same that I use with the audience of my weekly radio show. Since 1985, I have hosted the combination talk show and call-in program now called *Voices in the Family* on WHYY, the NPR affiliate in Philadelphia. Over the years, my many guests on the show have included mental health professionals and occasionally patients. But the real guests are those who call in to share their feelings and their experiences with other listeners.

I can still recall the day in August 1985, when Marty Moss-Coane, a producer at WHYY, asked me to host the program. I was frightened by the prospect of going on the air. I assumed the audience would not accept me because they had a two-year relationship with the previous host. In addition, I just "knew" the audience would be able to see inside me—to see my secrets and the parts of me that I was ashamed of. I assumed that everyone in the audience would be more knowledgeable than I. All my listeners, I was sure, were people with PhDs, with a thorough grounding in theoretical knowledge, and all much brighter than I. I was afraid I wouldn't even know how to answer their questions appropriately.

When I arrived at the station for my first show, Marty told me that my guest had been unable to come that night. I would have to do the interview by phone.

First show. No live guest. And now I had to face the audience alone!

Five minutes before the show began, I found myself sitting at a table in a studio alone with the interview questions in front of me. Marty adjusted the headphones. Before she left the studio, she put a mannequin's hand on the table for me to hold if things got bad during the show. As she was leaving the studio, she turned and said, "Have fun!"

She pulled the door closed behind her.

And there I sat in a small, darkened studio by myself. I was as frightened as I have ever been.

Somehow, I survived that show, and the next, and the next. Each week, the feedback from Marty and from Bill Siemering, the station manager, was more positive. But during those first few shows my anxiety persisted. I was fearful of the audience. That didn't really change until the end of the first month.

The month ended with an "open show" in which there were no guests, just the host and the audience. I talked a bit about my fears of the audience and what those fears were based on. I told my audience that I had been a poor student in school and had even done poorly in college. I talked about being ashamed of my lack of academic achievement and how I had finally struggled to make peace with my own mediocrity.

As soon as I began to talk about myself, I felt more comfortable and more intimate with the listeners. As those listeners called in, they shared parts of their lives, and I responded on a personal level.

Shortly thereafter, I invited Teddy Pendergrass—a friend and a well-known rhythm-and-blues singer—to be a guest on the show. Teddy had been paralyzed in a car accident. He and I both talked about our disabilities. And that was the first time I told my audience that I was a quadriplegic.

The accident happened to me on December 20, 1979, when I was thirty-three years old, on a highway sixty miles west of Philadelphia. At the time, I had a well-established career as a clinical psychologist. I was living comfortably with my family in a split-level suburban home in south Jersey. Athletics were important to me, especially golf—which I had learned in order to get closer to my father—and racquetball, which I played religiously twice a week.

In a few days it was going to be my tenth wedding anniversary. I had planned to buy a new Thunderbird for my wife, Sandy, and to bring it home as an anniversary surprise. The morning of the accident, I was driving out to my uncle's to pick up the car. At home were my two girls—Ali, who was six, and Debbie, who was five.

The last thing I remember seeing was a huge wheel in midair descending toward the roof of the car. I would later learn this one-hundred-pound wheel had broken loose from an oncoming trailer truck. It had bounced across the highway. I don't recall any anxiety or remember being hit. I do have one sharp memory of what I said a few moments after the accident. Someone was leaning over me, and I remember saying, "Call everybody I know—to come right away."

When the wheel smashed the roof of my car, the impact broke my neck and severed my spinal cord between the fifth and sixth cervical vertebrae. Had the break been higher, I would have been left with no movement at all. As it was, I could talk and I still had feeling in my face and shoulders. But at the moment my spinal cord was severed, I became a quadriplegic.

What followed were months of hospitalization, surgery, and therapy. I had become a living example of what most people secretly dread—to be stricken, paralyzed, and out of control. Like a newborn, I had to be fed, changed, held, nursed, and pampered. I constantly needed people around who loved me—not just family, but friends, professional colleagues, patients, nurses, visitors. My helplessness was obvious to all of them. They could easily see that I could not care for myself, could not control my own body, could not get along without them. I had to face the undeniable truth: If those people left me to myself, I would die.

At first I assumed I could not work again. Some former patients helped to change my mind. One of the couples I had been seeing before the accident became part of my support network. They came to see me frequently in the hospital. And about a month after I got out, they called and asked whether I was feeling good enough to go back to work yet. I said I was—and they came to see me as patients.

At the first session, I asked them whether they had wanted to resume therapy just to bolster my ego and make me feel good. The woman got very angry. She said, "I waited almost a year. We've still got work to do with you. Let's get to it."

I realized what I had to come to grips with. Despite seeing me in my helpless state, that couple still respected me. As a professional? As a man? I didn't know. At that point I didn't feel respect for myself and I wouldn't for many years. But I had to trust *their* respect for me.

And that began to raise many questions in my mind about what constitutes respect and what gets respect. I had always thought that broad shoulders, a good body, a good brain, and a good income—among other things—were what people respected. Instead I felt I was getting respect for my nakedness, my vulnerability, and my helplessness. Could that be true?

Six years later, with Teddy Pendergrass as my guest on a live radio show, I began to tell my audience of listeners what it meant to me to be a quadriplegic. I was again revealing my vulnerability. But this time, I was not speaking to a couple I had known before. I was speaking to tens of thousands of listeners.

Though I could not see the audience and I could only take some of their calls, their warm response seemed to rush into the studio. That response was something that went beyond words. Language had become a vehicle for communication—but it was only a vehicle. The emotions were conveyed by my nakedness and my vulnerability.

Once I was able to expose myself—to expose the parts I was ashamed of or embarrassed about—I felt safer, more intimate, and more loving. The words were part of the communication, but they didn't have anything to do with that interaction.

The more of me that I have shared with that audience over the years, the closer to them I have felt. At this point I feel very warm, even loving, toward them. I'm not quite clear who or what they represent to me, but I feel affection for them. I feel protective of *their* vulnerabilities, though most of them are people I've never even met.

The book in your hands is very much a book about feeling—how a talk-show host feels toward his audience; how parents feel toward their children, and children toward their parents. It's a book about how it feels to fall in love, to suffer a loss, to touch some hidden part of ourselves. It's about feelings of depression and helplessness, feelings of wholeness, and feelings that we have when we listen to each other's hearts.

Do you see why the words are so inadequate? What *is* the meaning of "wholeness"? What *do* we mean by "listening to the heart"? What language can convey what goes on between us when we are most broken, most loving, most depressed, or most joyous? It's certainly not the language of a "human science." But if not that, then what? The language of romance? Of spirituality? Of poetry and song?

My hope is that this book has a language that all of us, at some time in our lives, will use with each other. My wish is that you will find some words to use with your father, your mother, your children, or your spouse when other words have not been enough. And where I have described the communication among people, I hope you will try also to hear the silences, the waiting, the heartbeats. That, too, is part of the language of feeling.

Sometimes we are simply at a loss. A daughter has not really been able to talk to or hear her mother for many years. How does she begin? A husband and wife are fighting, and their child is behaving violently. Are there words that will heal this family? We become depressed and lonely; we want to feel that someone is close to us and cares; we want to be safe, sheltered, secure. Is there any way to communicate those needs?

Therapists rely on words to an extent. But whether they know it or not, therapists rely to a far greater extent on the power of the human spirit and they rely on the relationship for healing. Again and again, words fail. They fail to convey what happens when the tears begin. They fail to communicate as well as two people who reach out for each other's hands. Words fail when a family comes together for what they know will be the last time, to hug each other and to say good-bye. All words fail the articulate adults sitting in my office when a little girl suddenly sobs, "Daddy—don't leave me. Please don't leave me!"

No language can handle that. The messages explode. The power of the human spirit to sustain grief and loss and to renew itself with hope and courage defies all description.

And yet—here's the dilemma—the avenue to so many of these emotions is through the words that express the meaning of our relationships and the meaning of our lives. To a degree, our very understanding of the experience of life is shaped by the words. If we speak of the spirit instead of the id, we *become* more people-of-the-spirit than people-of-the-id. If we understand our lonely search as a search for wholeness rather than a march toward "integration of the self," then we are more likely to see ourselves become whole people rather than fragments that somehow fit together. If I speak of "listening to the heart" rather than "achieving cognitive understanding," I believe the bond that I share with my patients and that they share with each other will somehow be closer to the warm, beating heart than to the cool, more detached realm of cognitive understanding.

As a therapist, I feel comfortable at this point speaking to the spirit and the heart. I talk freely to my patients about their wholeness, as well as about their grief and their losses, their loves and their fears in life, and their denial of death. For me, these words have become the language of therapy as well as the language of living—the bridge between thought and feeling, between self and others, between family members who come into my office and the listeners who call in to *Voices in the Family*. I use these words with the hope that others, too, will use them to bridge some of the distance between our small wisdom and the unknowable reaches of the human spirit. Though words may be inadequate for that great task, they often provide a beginning.

PART ONE

❧

Our Parents

1

Listening to Our Parents

∾

As children, we develop an image of our parents—whether of a nurturing parent, an angry parent, or an all-powerful parent. The image becomes fixed in our mind. Sometimes that image resists change, despite the obvious biological changes that take place in both us and our parents.

If that image of a parent doesn't change very much as we become adults, often it's because we stop listening to our parents. When we don't hear them, we don't know what's in their hearts or how they're changing. When we're with them, we probably listen passively, often knowing in advance what we expect them to say. So the questions that we ask of our parents may begin and end with the usual amenities:

"How are you, Mom (or Dad)?"

"Oh, fine, and how are things with you?"

A colleague of mine told me that she'd always had this kind of relationship with her father. "But over the years," she said, "I started to realize that there were times when I really did want to know how my dad was. When he'd say, 'Oh, I'm fine,' that wasn't enough. I realized that the times when I truly wanted to know about him, I had to pursue the question further. I had to ask him specifically about his career or about some issue he'd mentioned before. I started to say, 'Dad, I want to know what's going on with you. Would you like to talk about it or not?' And about half the time he'd say, 'Yeah.'"

Often we have reflex answers for our parents. When I would ask my mother how she was doing and she said, "Fine," that, of course, was a reflex. She was not really telling me what was in her heart.

But when I really want to know how someone's doing, I have to think about *what* I really want to know. Do I want to know about her health? Do I want to find out whether she's worried about something? Do I want her to tell me about changes in her life?

A question is a hunger. It says, "Feed me. I want something—for my intellect, for my spirit, for my emotions. I want to express my interest in you and my love for you."

If you respect yourself enough to ask the question, stay with it until you get an answer. You can ask without being intrusive—but respect your own need to make contact, to touch. If you're bold enough to open the door, go in! Don't stay outside.

Allen and his wife Jacqui came to see me at a time when Allen was having difficulty with his job and his studies. Both he and Jacqui complained about their marriage. There was a good deal of arguing going on. Jacqui said Allen didn't understand her needs. Allen complained that he didn't feel Jacqui was supportive enough of him, and this angered him.

Allen went home to his parents' house for Thanksgiving. Jacqui was spending the holiday with her family, and they wouldn't see each other for a few days.

Allen's mother, who was in her early seventies, was a nurturing person. Allen identified with her and felt close to her in many ways. Allen's father was a military man—strong, tough, always in control—who expected the house to be orderly and meals to be served on time. Growing up, Allen had naturally looked to his father as a role model. Like his father, Allen could not find a way to be tender and vulnerable and to show his emotions—for them, this was not acceptable in a man. Allen had always felt protective of his mother, and he'd wanted to be tender toward her in a way that his father was not. As she aged, he felt even more protective of her. But he didn't know how to show his tenderness.

When Allen went to his parents' home on this visit, he was feeling needy and he expected some tender loving care. The whole family was together, and Allen's mother was spending a lot of time in the kitchen. That was where Allen tried to talk to her about what was going on in his life.

When Allen came back after that holiday, he was frustrated. During the next session when he and Jacqui came to see me, Allen talked about how angry he was at his mother. "You know, she seemed not to care," he said. "First she would ask me a question, and then she'd change the subject and talk about something else. A couple of hours later, she would repeat the same question as if she'd never asked me before."

"Did you ask her how *she* was feeling?" I asked.

"Yes," he replied. "I asked her how she was—and she said she'd been feeling pretty good."

"Did you ask her whether it was taxing for her—preparing food for all these people?"

He shook his head.

"Did you ask her how she felt about this stage of her life?"

"No, I didn't."

"Did you ask her how it felt to be seventy?"

He shook his head again.

"My God," he said finally, "I didn't see her as a regular woman. I never have. She's just always been my mom—who was there to nurture me. I didn't see her as a person. I feel so guilty."

When Allen asked his mother how she was and she said she was feeling "pretty good," neither of them was getting past the amenities.

Allen had a lot of noise in his head. All his preoccupation with his work and studies combined with his need for TLC drowned out anything his mother was saying. That's no crime, of course. We all have noise like that, and it interferes with our listening. But I know that when the noise in my head begins to interfere, I have to talk about it, and then I'm able to listen better.

If Allen felt so needy that he couldn't hear his mother, what I would encourage him to say is, "Mom, I'm really feeling vulnerable and unhappy. Whatever TLC you have available, I'd sure like some right now."

What could make anyone feel better than to be asked for help and nurture? When Allen was more open, his mother would also be. It would be easier for her to speak if Allen talked about what was going on inside him: his talking, and showing his vulnerability, would make it feel safe for her to talk, too.

By the end of the session with Allen and Jacqui, I realized that perhaps I had made Allen feel guilty. So I asked him whether I had. Was I being too aggressive?

He said that I was, that he felt as if I were reprimanding him.

I thought, "Well, why did I reprimand him?" And realized, the person I was *really* reprimanding was me. I had never asked those questions of my mother. And now I was making Allen feel guilty for not asking his mother.

So we both talked to our mothers.

After Allen had talked to his mother, he went through a period of mild depression. He had to give up the hope of getting something that he'd never gotten—namely, the assurance that his mother would be able to take away his pain and confusion and to make it "all better." He finally realized that his mother was a seventy-year-old woman who needed nurturing herself. That image of the mother he had in his head finally dissipated and gave way to that of a seventy-year-old woman who was aging, growing more fragile and needy. He said he felt somewhat depressed over the loss of this image, distorted though it was, but the idea of nurturing his mother felt good.

Once he realized that nobody in his life could make things "all better," his marriage improved. He took more responsibility for his anger and his pain. He and Jacqui argued less because he was demanding less of her. In addition, despite the fact that the stress in his life hadn't changed, he was able to hear Jacqui more clearly. This is something Jacqui experienced as nurturing—just his listening.

When I finally talked to my mother, it was about many things. How it felt to grow older. How she saw my father and me. Whether death seemed less fearful to her now than it had when she was younger.

It was a good conversation—the kind we had never had before. It helped me see her more clearly as a person. I felt closer to her.

Some time later, I accompanied my parents when they went to sign the papers on the purchase of a condominium. They were moving out of the house my sister and I had grown up in. My mother seemed a bit nervous and sad. As we were sitting at the table, I felt her hand slide into mine. It felt good to both of us. I think this is something she wouldn't have thought of doing and I wouldn't have tolerated, had we not shared that recent conversation. It would have been too uncomfortable for both of us.

Before she signed the papers, she whispered to me, "Danny, be sure they put up the new wallpaper."

I heard it as, "Danny, *I* need *you* now."

And she continued to hold my hand while she signed the papers.

It was a tender and bittersweet moment for all of us.

2

Understanding Our Relationship with Our Parents

∾

Imagine that three moviegoers have just seen different parts of the same film:

In the first part, the young heroine escapes poverty and deprivation, marries a handsome, successful young man, and has two lovely children. Part one ends as the happy young couple walks hand in hand through a field of wildflowers while the children romp in the tall grass.

At the beginning of part two, the older child is killed in a tragic accident. Husband and wife become estranged, their marriage ends in divorce. The surviving child becomes lonely, distant, and unhappy. Part two ends as the heroine attempts suicide.

In part three, the woman recovers and begins a new life; she and her daughter become loving companions. The heroine has a number of unsatisfying romantic relationships—the loss of her earlier happiness is always present—but by the end of the film she is more at peace with her life.

Now, in this imaginary scenario, suppose all three moviegoers meet afterward to compare their reactions.

"What a happy movie," says the first viewer. "The woman got everything she wanted."

"I disagree. It was tragic," says the second. "Those people are doomed to misery."

"Not at all!" says the third. "The woman lost a great deal—but her life is still very rich."

The three viewers look at each other critically. And each is wondering the same thing about the other: What's the *matter* with this person? How could anybody *be so wrong?*

An apocryphal story, of course—but it says something about the way each of us sees the world. We are each looking at different portraits—portraits we carry inside, that began to be painted at the moment we are conceived by our parents. Broad strokes are placed on those portraits-of-the-world by our early experience, both with our parents and with our loved ones. Peers and other significant people add further brushstrokes. For most of us, the paint dries early. And after the paint dries, that's the portrait we carry.

That portrait is a picture of how we view the world, how we view people, men versus women, and whether life is to be enjoyed or survived. The painting can be dominated by bright yellows and reds, or by somber grays and browns. (Of course, those portraits have little to do with our real lives, because our real lives are a combination of all those colors.)

And what are the portraits that our parents carry with *them?* Do we understand what colors *their* world is painted in? When we're painting portraits of our world, do we use the same brushes that our parents used?

My late sister and my brother-in-law were very successful in business. They had always managed money well, and were financially secure.

But my mother worried about them constantly. Why were they spending so much? Were they putting away enough for a rainy day? What would happen if their business collapsed? My mother worried about things that rarely concerned my sister and brother-in-law. Nothing could get my mother to stop worrying about them—and of course we would not want to change her; her worrying was part of her love. But where did her concern come from?

Well, the portrait my mother painted in childhood was tinged with grim browns and beiges because *her* parents (my grandmother and grandfather) came out of czarist Russia at the most frightening of times. They emigrated to the United States and started a family; they had four children and went through terrible struggles trying to make a living. Then, just when things seemed to be getting more comfortable for them, the Depression hit. Once again they were struggling desperately to survive.

So my mother carried a portrait of the world that she received from my grandmother. My mother saw the world as a place under siege—since my grandmother's world was under siege. Growing up in a family where insecurity was always part of the picture, my mother could not even recognize the secure world that my sister and brother-in-law had painted for themselves. Their feelings of financial security could not affect the way she saw the world. After seventy years of life, my mother's portrait was not going to be altered significantly by somebody else's bankbook.

As young children, we're likely to see the world much as our parents do, in similar shades of color. But usually that worldview changes as we grow older, have our own experiences, and begin painting the world from our own palette of colors.

Of course, children are watching different parts of the movie than their parents did. *Our* lives start somewhere in our parents' adult years, when they're already well along in their journey. By the time we show up on the scene, they may already see the world as very frightening, and if they do, their fondest wish is to protect us from the dangers of that world. On the other hand, their experience of life or their outlook may have convinced them that the world is a welcoming place, filled with opportunities for growth, adventure, and exploration.

When parents see the world as a fearful, risky place, the family is usually a closed system. Barricades go up to protect the family from a hostile-looking environment. "We"—the people inside the family—are safe and protected as long as "they"—the outside influences—are kept at bay. In this type of closed family system, children grow up seeing the world in terms of "us" versus "them." In an extremely closed system, outsiders are generally regarded with mistrust, and even friends can be threatening if they bring too much change into the family. In a closed system there is clearly a "we/they" approach to the world.

What's it like for a child to grow up in a closed system?

Let's say Jill brings home a note from her teacher that says she's misbehaving. She's going to be held back unless her attitude improves.

In the closed family, there are likely to be "blind" reactions to this kind of intrusion. One reaction is to deny the information and say there's just something wrong with the teacher—*"That teacher is picking on my child!"* Another type of "blind" reaction is to assume automatically that the teacher is right. Blame is turned on the child: *"What's wrong with you? Why can't you pay attention? Do you want to be held back?"*

The first reaction is a refusal to weigh data from the teacher—to get real information about what's going on in the classroom. The second reaction is equally blind: the family refuses to allow input from the child. In neither case does the parent explore, listen to people, find out what's really going on, and then react in a measured way, based on his or her own experience. In a closed system, the parent just reacts.

It's years later now, and Jill has grown up. She's had many experiences on her own—some of which threatened her parents and distanced her from them. Yet her relationship with her parents has remained essentially unchanged.

Now embarked on a career, the older Jill has just been passed over for her first raise. She comes home one weekend and tells her parents how disappointed and confused she feels. Her parents have a reaction very similar to the one they had had years before: "Your boss doesn't know what he's doing," they tell her. Or, "You should have put in more hours—then you would have gotten the raise."

Despite all that Jill has done on her own, she hasn't changed the system a bit. She has gone out into the world, made her own way. Her parents may have disapproved, or they may have tried to protect her. But nothing *she* has done—or will do—changes her parents' view of the world.

The best Jill can hope for is to understand better what makes her parents respond the way they do. To the extent that she can do that, she can give up trying to change the system—which, after all, *can't* be changed. At the same time, she can be true to her own portrait of the world, painted in the colors that she sees clearly for herself.

—⁓—

At the other end of the spectrum is an "open" family system, where family members can tolerate being confused; they are more receptive to learning, growing, and dealing with the outside world. Parents in an open system are, of course, concerned about their children, but they neither willfully resist what their children try to do, nor do they willfully try to change them. They can relate to what outsiders *really* say and do, rather than make assumptions about others' motives and intentions.

I worked with one couple that was quite conservative in their own lifestyle, yet their family was very open. Bruce, a man in his mid-sixties, was a surgeon; his fifty-five-year-old wife Elizabeth was a mental health professional. At the time I was seeing them, they had just said good-bye to both of their daughters.

Beth, their twenty-year-old, had dropped out of college, bought a plane ticket to Paris, and left for a year with five hundred dollars in her pocket. Bruce and Elizabeth were concerned about the usual things: Would she have enough to live on? Would she find a safe place to live in Paris? But they were also excited for her. They never tried to stop her. As she left, they told her, "Keep us posted. Tell us how it goes. We're here if you need us."

Their second daughter, eighteen-year-old Marianne, made arrangements to go to Colombia during the first summer after her freshman year. This was just when the Colombian courts were extraditing drug lords to the United States—the worst possible time for U.S. citizens to visit that country. Bruce and Elizabeth didn't want Marianne to go, and they told her so. But she decided to go anyway. Her parents didn't withhold the money or try to stop her. They were frightened, and they knew they would be frightened all summer. But they didn't resist her.

At one point, Bruce said to me, "You know, I've done many things in my life and I don't have any regrets. I consider my life an adventure. If the adventure is not lived, then life isn't worth living."

So that's one view: life as an adventure. At the other extreme is the view that life is difficult and you'd better do everything you can to be prepared.

Most of us grew up in a family system that was at neither extreme, but somewhere in between. If your family system was more closed, you probably felt that your role was to be the loyal son or daughter, to do what was expected. Experimenting and adventuring had to be postponed until you left home and were on your own.

But some children in a closed system begin to resist it early. They begin to experiment openly in their adolescent years. They're really "scouts" for the family—going out into the world, adventuring—and they often serve a purpose for the family. The closed family may depend on its "scout" to bring outside culture into the system.

It is a warm summer day. The window is open; a light breeze comes into the office. The five family members—mother, father, and three adult children—seem nervous and uncomfortable.

Andrew, thirty-four, began therapy because he had experienced failure in a sequence of relationships. Frustrated and angry with what he saw as a pattern, he sought help.

Andrew's parents, Chuck and Martha, are a couple in their mid-sixties. They were divorced when he was eight years old. Neither Andrew nor his sister and brother ever knew why their parents were divorced.

I ask Chuck and Martha about their divorce. How did it come about? What were the causes? Why did they decide to separate?

It is apparent from what Andrew has told me that both parents grew up in closed family systems. There were many expectations placed on the children, and much loyalty was expected of them. Chuck's household was a patriarchy: the law of the household when he was growing up was in his father's hands. Chuck had assumed that in the family he created, he would rule the way his father did. Martha came from a matriarchy; she had learned from *her* mother that women control the household. Andrew's parents brought these rigid—and very different—expectations of their own systems into their marriage.

The parents are tense as we talk about the life they shared many years before. Finally, Chuck recalls an important conversation that he had with his wife when Andrew was just four years old. He says he argued with her over the issue of whether Andrew should go to nursery school. Andrew's father does not recall the content of the argument, but he knows the outcome. Martha got her way.

When Martha is asked to remember that argument, she has only a vague memory. She doesn't even recall who won. "But as I think about it," she says, "I have a vague sense that the argument was very important. I wasn't aware of it then, but I am now."

Sitting in my office thirty years later, Chuck recalls this as the moment when he realized he would have to leave Martha. In his view a man should not lose an argument to his wife. In losing the argument, Chuck felt that he had disappointed his own father—that his father would no longer respect him. The only way Chuck could reclaim *his* father's respect was by leaving his wife.

And Andrew—was he trying to perpetuate the system? Was this why all his relationships "fell apart"? In a rigid family system, a child may grow up feeling guilty, fearful, and ashamed and never know why. As we see that system for what it is—as we recognize its inflexible rules and regulations—we may see more clearly the portrait of the world that we carry around with us because of that system. But to the extent that we can see what *we* want, as distinct from what the system demands, we can separate our *selves* from our *parents*—*and* accept each other's differences.

Along with the portraits of the world that we inherited from our parents, we also have pictures *of* our parents. But many of these pictures are delusions: we began painting them when we were four, or ten, or sixteen years old, and they have not changed at all over the years.

I am reminded of a conversation I had with a man who described his mother as "Attila the Hun." I asked the man to invite his mother to a session. He did so.

Helen was a short, plump, white-haired woman in her early seventies. She wore a brightly patterned dress and held her purse on her lap during the first part of the session. When she felt more comfortable, she set the purse aside.

Earlier, Dennis had described the humiliation he had felt as a young boy whenever his mother's shrill, strident voice called him home to dinner. He remembered how his friends had laughed at him. Dennis was ashamed of his mother and secretly angry.

Now, with Dennis and Helen both in the same room, I asked Helen to tell me something about her childhood. She began to describe the neighborhood she had grown up in during the 1920s. She recalled how she and the other children had all played together in the street. But Helen's mother was the only mom who worked all day, and she was never home in time for dinner. When all the other moms were calling their kids to come home, no one called Helen. Every night, she felt hurt, lonely, and aban-doned—and she swore her children would never experience that pain. By the time Attila the Hun finished telling Dennis that story, he was holding her hand and they were both crying.

There were other things, as well, that Dennis heard for the first time during that session. He had complained that his mother was overeating. He was annoyed that she didn't watch her diet. In Dennis's view, it was "suicidal" for a woman of that age to keep putting on weight the way she did.

When we talked about that issue, Helen recalled that her own mother had also been overweight. Her best memory of her mother—the woman she saw so rarely—was a view of her standing in the kitchen with her stomach pressed against the edge of the counter as she prepared meals for the family. As Helen's mother worked, her stomach rubbed against the edge of the countertop. Helen recalled exactly how the apron was worn thin around the middle.

I asked Helen, "And how is your apron?"

Helen gave me a big grin and said, "Mine is worn out there, too—just like my mother's."

I caught Dennis's eye. "Some 'suicidal,' huh?"

He laughed ruefully.

Later on, when I saw Dennis again in a private session, he described what the experience of listening to his mother was like for him. And his description was vivid. "It was like an empty shell," he said, "being filled up with reality."

I think it's difficult to talk to our parents as if they are real human beings if we have nothing other than a distorted view. As another family therapist once said to me, "I'm always startled to meet the parents of people who have described their parents ahead of time. The parents *never* have fangs, and there's *always* something in common between the parent and child, however estranged they may be."

I have to agree.

In twenty years as a family therapist, I have yet to meet any parent who has fangs.

When you become an adult, the nature of your family system becomes clearer to you. As you have more experiences and discover how your family compares to others', you can gain some objectivity about the system you grew up in and how it works.

And what is your role now?

To watch—and to be. You can't change the system in your family of origin. Of course, your own portrait of the world is painted differently than your parents'; you are using fresh colors. If your family system was very closed, you may be the "scout," the one who dares to do things that your mother, father, or even your siblings would never do. And if you are starting a family of your own, you have the opportunity to raise your children in a different system if you want to. But as different as you are, as different as your new family is, you can't change the system you grew up in.

What you can do is understand the system better. You can ask your mother and father more about themselves, find out their worldview, find out what colors they have on their palettes, what part of the movie they've seen. You can discover what makes them feel secure and what frightens them. You can ask what adventures they've had—and where they encountered land mines.

But when you discover your parents' fears, please don't try to talk them out of those fears. Because that's being disrespectful of them and their experience.

3

What Happens When Our Parents Have Crises?

∾

It was a beautiful spring evening in early June when I visited the University of Pennsylvania campus. Along shady, tree-lined Locust Walk, it was beginning to look like summer, with students in shorts and polo shirts headed for tennis courts or hanging around classroom doors.

In McNeil Hall, two hundred people had crowded into an open forum of the radio show that would later be broadcast on WHYY. The subject of the evening, midlife issues, was at least two decades away for the students outside on Locust Walk. My guest was Ed Monte, a senior staff psychologist at the Marriage Council of Philadelphia.

As the program got under way and a number of people from the audience began to speak, I noticed that the subject of the program very quickly turned from midlife issues to parental issues.

It makes sense. Midlife is a time when we confront our own mortality through our parents. We become aware of the crises in our own lives as our parents confront illness, aging, and death.

But that's always the case—isn't it? As children, we experience adulthood through our parents. Through them we learned about commitment to marriage, about how to argue with a loved one (or how to avoid it!), about how to manage a career and many more "lessons" of living. In midlife, it's through them we experience aging and death.

One woman in the audience introduced herself by saying she was "not really aware of being in a midlife crisis. I'm past forty, childless, and I have a career. My father is a diabetic. He lives about seven hundred miles away. He's an amputee.

"He now has to use a walker," she went on. "I know this is hard for him, but he never talks about what's going on with him. I guess for the past couple of years I've expected him to die. I've thought, well, the next trip home, he's not going to be there—though that may seem a harsh way to put it.

"I want to deal with his *end*-of-the-life crisis, I guess. I think he must be having one—or else he's very courageous. He's a very reserved person who doesn't talk about his feelings.

"I'm not sure what my question is," the woman continued. "'Midlife crisis' doesn't resonate with me—but I know that there are some areas of my life where I'm stuck. And I know that a lot of it has to do with the father that's in me. And I want to engage him in conversation."

I asked her to visualize a scenario that might be very frightening to her—to imagine that she and her father were sitting together, and they had exactly one hour with each other. Just one hour. And her father was there to listen to her without answering.

"What would you say?" I asked.

I realized that the woman couldn't reveal everything that she *would* say to her father—not in front of two hundred people. But I had a point to make, a thought for her to carry from that room: that the pain she was feeling wasn't her father's; it was her own. The past she had to deal with in order to help her get unstuck had to do with her feelings about the loss of her father, her feelings about her own dying. Through that work, the father inside her can be liberated, and she can see that her father is just a man.

Any crisis that our parents go through forces us to deal with these issues within ourselves. We owe it to our parents and ourselves to ask, "What does this mean to me? How does it make me feel? Can I acknowledge my fears, vulnerabilities, hurts?"

If we don't ask these questions of ourselves, if we don't take responsibility for our own feelings, then we're at risk of manipulating our parents to help us avoid feeling these things. For example, if I have fears and anxieties about my mother's aging and my fear of losing her but don't deal with these feelings and take responsibility for them, I might pressure her to see different doctors for more interventions in her health, to change her diet, to take more pills. I could wind up harassing this poor woman so I don't have to be alone with my own anxiety.

If this is true, not only won't I be able to hear her and her issues but I won't be able to *experience* her either. To experience her is to feel her pain and my pain; her sense of helplessness and my sense of helplessness; my hunger for her touch, and hers for mine. As one patient said to me, "I would like to talk to my mother, but I'm afraid she won't be able to hear my heart." To experience my mother is to hear her heart.

Here's a woman who's at a critical stage of her life, struggling with issues of dependency and independence. And I come along to manipulate her and tell her what to do. What a sad state of affairs!

The woman who spoke *knew* that her father was becoming increasingly dependent. His health was failing—yes, possibly he could see his own death approaching. He was feeling frightened and vulnerable. Because of her anxiety about "his" crisis, they were both at risk. How would it feel to him at that point in his life to have his daughter tell him what she thought he needed— to be less reserved, more open and expressive of his love? At the very least, it would be a blow to his independence and dignity. And she would be doing it to avoid looking at the painful issues inside herself!

Of course, she would not be doing this intentionally—but it could happen. I wanted her to know her own pain, her own anxiety, so she would not unwittingly punish her father for being unable to express the fear and vulnerability he may have been feeling at this time.

Crises in our parents are terribly frightening and painful. One issue that makes any crisis more painful is the loneliness involved. Often, the parent and the child are both dealing with the same crisis, although each of us is dealing with this crisis in his own way. Of course, I can't take responsibility for making my mother or father feel less lonely during the crisis. But I can take responsibility for my own feelings and say something like, "Dad, I feel frightened. I'd like to be able to help you, but I feel helpless. It makes me fear your death and mine."

To talk about my vulnerability doesn't diminish me, but it allows me to feel more connected with him and opens the door for him to talk about *his* vulnerability.

There's another advantage in saying things this way. When we do, we're also saying, "I'm talking about what goes on *inside* me. Therefore, it's safe to talk about what goes on *inside* you—if you would like."

And because you've liberated yourself from your own "secret fears" and anxieties, you truly are more available to listen to your parents and really hear them.

When I talked to the woman in McNeil Hall about her father's crisis, my hope was that she would later be able to listen to him. Given an hour with him—given just ten minutes, for that matter—I hoped she could talk about her own fears. And maybe, just maybe, she would make it safe for him to talk about himself, his life, and his death.

Often, times of crisis are also those times when we most need to forgive our parents. I recall a consultation I had with a family that was dealing with the illness of their thirty-year-old daughter, Jeanette, who had multiple sclerosis. Her older sister, Peggy, was a divorced executive who had brought in the family for a single therapy session.

Peggy wanted to fix this family; she wanted them all to become stronger so they could join forces to help Jeanette; and she wanted Jeanette to help herself by becoming more active and achieving more. But Peggy's special target for healing was her father—a frail-looking man who sat with folded hands next to his wife on the sofa.

The father was an alcoholic who had stopped drinking about ten years before. Peggy was angry at her father for his alcoholism; she had always felt he was the one who could rescue the family, though of course he never did. Now she asked him in a very aggressive way to talk about his alcoholism. She wanted to know why he drank. "What did it feel like—not being *there* when we were growing up?" she asked him.

When her father said, "I feel guilty about that," Peggy replied, "Perhaps you deserve to."

Her father shrank even further into himself.

I turned to Peggy and said, "Tell me about the father you always wanted."

She described a man who could, in fact, rescue the family. The father she had always wanted was a man who was chemically sober and emotionally strong. That was the kind of man she wanted right now at the head of the family, to help them all through this crisis.

I asked, "Peggy, when did that other father die for you?"

"When I was fourteen."

"Did you ever have a funeral for that other man?"

"No," she shook her head. "I never have."

Pointing to her father, I asked whether she could ever forgive that man, her real father, for not being the father who had died. She replied quite honestly that she didn't know, but she would like to try.

Then I turned to her father and asked him about his drinking. What had it been like for him all those years?

He was able to talk about how he had hated himself and how he felt he had wasted thirty years of his life that could never be retrieved.

Those were the feelings he had now. But before Peggy could hear about his feelings, she had to forgive the man on the sofa for not being the father she wanted him to be. The image of a strong, sober father had to die before she could experience the man who sat in front of her with folded hands.

When our parents have crises, they do not become different from what they were. They don't become stronger, more competent, or healthier. We can't change them—and we can't help them by being angry at their refusal to change. If we want to listen and experience what that crisis is like for them, we first need to forgive them. If they know they will not be accused, blamed, or reminded of their failures, perhaps then they will feel that they have permission to say what's in their hearts. And then, perhaps, we can hear them.

4

Coping with a Parent's Addiction

෨

Whenever I schedule a show where alcoholism and addiction are going to be discussed, I know I'm going to get a flood of calls. The callers will be children of alcoholic parents; alcoholics who are currently in programs, struggling to make it "one day at a time" (the Alcoholics Anonymous credo); and spouses who are striving to hold their families and their lives together while a mate succumbs daily or periodically to the effects of addiction.

Addiction has many forms, but I think all forms have at least one thing in common: *People take in things from the outside and become dependent on them.*

We all have internal hungers that we need to satisfy—hungers that might be related to loneliness, emptiness, or agitation. And in the addicted person a hunger is out of control. In some instances, the loss of control is increased by a genetic or physiologic need for a substance. But whether or not the physical need exists, there is an emotional hunger that begs to be satisfied—a hunger to feel safe, a hunger to be known, or a hunger to feel whole. Or, perhaps, just a hunger to be.

Why is addiction so prevalent? Why is there so much of it in our culture, in our times?

I am reminded of a conversation that I had with a food addict—someone who has binges of compulsive eating. She told me, "The only time I feel calm is when I'm eating."

Alcoholics and drug addicts often use similar descriptions. There is a calmness that comes when they drink or take drugs— a calmness that momentarily "cures" the inner agitation, the emptiness that so many people feel at other times.

We live in a society that values the myth of independence: the Declaration of Independence, a keystone of our free society, is a testament to that myth. The price we pay for pursuing this myth of independence is that we can't acknowledge our dependency needs. We can't even use the word *dependent*. We use fancy new psychological words, like *interdependence*.

One of my greatest struggles after the accident in which I broke my neck was dealing with my dependency needs— accepting the fact that I am a dependent man. I think my loss of independence was more difficult for me to come to grips with than my loss of function.

Such a rigid denial of dependency comes up frequently in our society. So much of our improved technology and our mechanistic advancements—cars, computers, ATM machines, cell phones, and so on—help us to feel more "independent." But despite all the modern mechanisms of independence, we still have dependency needs. So how do we acknowledge those needs?

All our needs have to be acknowledged one way or another. I think the increase in addiction can be attributed, at least in part, to the dependency needs that must be acknowledged somewhere, somehow. When we become dependent on food, gambling, alcohol, drugs, or work, I think we are finding ways to say, "In addition to other things, there's a part of me that's a dependent person."

Others of us may become addicted to addicts; we become compulsive caretakers for those who are substance abusers or have other kinds of addictions. One of the by-products of growing up in a family in which there's been addiction is that the children become addicted to taking care of people. The caretakers are as addicted to "fixing things" or "fixing people" or "making things right" as addicts are to their substance. Like the addicts they care for, caretakers feel withdrawal symptoms when they stop fixing, changing, trying to cure—and, instead, just "let things go." The anxiety, fear, and mistrust that they feel when letting go are similar to what the addict feels when he lets go of his substance.

A psychotherapist I know, who I worked with in an addiction program in South Philadelphia, calls alcohol and drugs "do-it fluids." The label is apt. Alcohol and other addictive substances "do it" for us—allow us to feel more powerful and more expressive, allow us to *feel whole* while we are under the influence.

If we have an addiction, what we yearn for is the "calmness" (as my patient described it) of satisfying that addiction. We want to feel like a person who is in control, and addiction gives the illusion that we are. As a "hunger" arises in us, we reach for the substance, or we reach out for emotional contact, or we repeat the addictive behavior that makes us feel calm and in control. But whenever that all-powerful feeling of being in control begins to slip away, the emptiness returns.

What does the child experience in an environment where there is an addicted parent?

In such families the child is involuntarily exposed to the disturbed thinking that is part of the family system. The child sees the color blue; he says, "That's blue." But everyone else in the family says, "No, you're wrong, that's not blue!" What is the child supposed to believe? That he's crazy—or the family is crazy? Neither is acceptable. The child adopts the family's "reality" of not-blue, but the reality he's adopted never really fits inside. So a child who grows up in a family like this sees his reality one way and at the same time knows it's not real.

Paul, a man I treated, had grown up in an alcoholic family. By the time Paul was ten years old, his father had left the family and the boy had become the caretaker of his alcoholic mother. He recalled the first sight that greeted him every day when he arrived home from school. As he came in the back door, he saw his mother's hair spread over her arm on the kitchen table. She was lying on the table, passed out. Paul knew that he had to help her upstairs into bed and that he had to make dinner for his younger sister and himself. This daily routine became automatic.

"When I was ten," Paul told me, "I assumed this was my life. This was my reality. At the same time, I realized that none of my friends lived like this. I knew something was terribly wrong, but everyone in my family said, 'Nothing's wrong. Your mother is just under stress.' I couldn't trust my own reality—I couldn't trust myself. It was twenty years before I knew I was hurt, burdened, and angry at my mother."

What this man described to me is the experience of family members who exist in the world of an alcoholic. Inside each person is a part that knows what truth is and another part that believes "nothing's really wrong." That's what is meant by collusion: the whole family experiences a distortion in the same way. They collude with each other to make life bearable in the face of an overwhelming disturbance, because the truth is too frightening. Therefore, nobody can trust their own sense of reality.

To grow up in a family in which there's addiction is to grow up in a family in which all of the emotional energy is focused either on the addiction or on denial that the addiction exists. What that suggests is that children are at the very least overlooked and at the very worst emotionally malnourished and/or abused. At the same time, they believe if they can do things better, the parent will actually stop drinking, will be less depressed.

When a child is exposed to a situation that's out of control, he believes that he has some ability to control it. The child thinks, "If I'm good, Mom might not beat me." The deepest hope is, "If I'm good, maybe Mom will take care of me."

One reason this happens is that the child often is blamed for what happens in the family. The parent may use phrases like, "If you had set the table better, I wouldn't be so upset" or "If you played with different friends, I wouldn't have to worry about you" or "If you did better in school, I wouldn't be so disappointed."

The effect of this kind of criticism on the child is to make him feel grandiose about his own powers. He starts to feel that if only he were perfect, then things at home would be calm.

In other words: "If I'm always perfect, I'll have a parent."

Of course, the child is never perfect, and the parent rarely changes behavior, so the child grows up not only struggling to be perfect but also feeling like a failure.

When I work with the adult children of alcoholics, a number of themes frequently recur. Some of the "adult children" have a sense of inadequacy and guilt-feelings of incompetence from not being able to control things at home adequately. For others there's anger at being abused or neglected. Oftentimes there's anger at the "sober" parent for not protecting the child.

In addition, the grandiosity still exists: "I know there are answers out there. If I can find them, I'll be able to fix my mother or father." Or, "If I read more, do more, try harder, I'll come closer to finding those answers at last."

Frequently, people who come to therapy—or those who join groups like Alcoholics Anonymous or Alanon—are still looking for answers: they want more effective and efficient ways to make their parents sober people. And sometimes they come to these groups with just a generalized sense of bitterness and cynicism about the way the world works. After they've been in treatment for a while, somehow the anger and cynicism give way to hurt, sadness, and grief. Their sadness is over lost parents and lost childhood, but there's also sadness about the legacy they carry. (Many adult children of alcoholics, by the time they seek help, already have either become alcoholics or have married alcoholics.)

Vince Di Pasquale, one of the guests I interviewed on *Voices in the Family,* was the founder of Starting Point, a rehabilitation program for alcoholics in southern New Jersey. Vince himself is the child of an alcoholic. When he was describing the children of alcoholics to our listeners, he removed any mention of the specific addictive substance from his description.

"As I define addiction," Vince said, "it's what happens to a person who lives in fear, guilt, and dependency."

One of the callers on that show was a woman in her early thirties who said her mother was an overeater and her father was an alcoholic who'd had a drinking problem for at least fifteen years.

"I wasn't abused physically as a child," said the caller. "However, I really didn't get a lot of attention. I've gone through therapy myself—the whole bit about 'low self-esteem'—and I'm finally realizing I'm okay. But I've come from a very abnormal, sick family, and I have to work harder than the normal person to 'think healthy.' Now I'm at the point where I really want to talk to my father about it. But he's seventy years old and he's very sick."

I asked the caller whether her father was still drinking.

"Yes. I can't get up my strength to approach him. I don't know what to say. I've got so much anger in me."

"What is it you want to say to him?"

"I just want him to stop drinking. I want him to dry out. I want him to go into counseling. I just wish he liked himself, so he wouldn't treat himself so badly. He's killing himself, and that's a painful thing to watch."

But was it really the daughter's task to get her father to stop drinking? She thought it was—after all, it's a job she had held for many years. And she was understandably frustrated. But amazingly, after all these years of failure, she still hadn't given up. She was still doing battle with him. Surely *now* (she told herself) as he approached the end of his life, he could see that it was time to stop!

"It's hard to say this," Vince replied, "but your father has a *right* to drink if he wants to." Vince recalled his own experience with an alcoholic who had refused treatment. One afternoon when he was working in a halfway house, he had talked steadily for two and a half hours to an addict, trying to convince the man to enter a rehabilitation program. After observing this process, Vince's co-counselor and mentor finally took him aside and said: "Vince, the man *wants* to drink! *Leave him the hell alone!*"

"I learned my lesson," said Vince. "I can't save anyone who doesn't want to be saved. And something I would suggest to you—something that I had to deal with myself as an 'adult child' of an alcoholic—is to be able to get a hold on those anger feelings. Maybe through some group such as Alanon, you will be able to release those feelings, to get them out. Maybe you can even practice talking to your father with somebody who's healthy."

Vince described a practice he follows called "reconstructing your family"—going into the family of origin and reconstructing it healthily for yourself. "But this doesn't mean changing your father," he went on. "Just the opposite. It means being able to release those feelings—to let them out—but with healthy people."

As Vince suggested to this caller, being with "healthy people" is essential in the recovery process. Anyone who grows up with addiction has the kind of invalidating experiences of being told that "blue is not blue"—you're told that a drunk parent is not drunk, or the fear that you feel is not fear, or that abusive punishment is really a sign of love. This invalidation of your emotions and your experiences induces a kind of trance; you go into a fog.

But what can you do to get out of the fog? Where can you find validation for your feelings? You won't get that validation from your family, because your family is unsafe (unless everyone has successfully gone through treatment). So you have to find a reconstructed "family" of healthy people. That family might be loved ones, friends' parents, aunts, uncles, an organization like Adult Children of Alcoholics (ACOA) or Alanon—or it might begin with your relationship with a therapist. You need those healthy people to confirm that *what you feel is true.*

If you're the child of an addicted parent, most of your life has been devoted to finding yourself by trying to heal your parents, their marriage, their addiction; or by trying to heal your sick siblings; or by trying to solve other family problems related to dependency and addiction. When you are able to release your feelings in therapy, among healthy people, or in a recovery group, you can begin to find yourself by looking inside rather than by looking outside.

As I'd listened to the woman who was talking to Vince, I had begun to have an image of her and her father as partners repeating the same steps over and over again in a tired, monotonous dance. For years she'd been trying to control her father's drinking. Her father had resisted. The daughter had felt inadequate and angry. Her father had felt guilty. In this dance, they had circled each other again and again until the daughter was almost exhausted. I began to wonder how they could change the steps—what could be done in their relationship that would be new.

I encouraged her to try to get to know her father apart from his drinking.

"What do you mean?" she asked.

"Well, what kind of man is he, other than just an alcoholic? Does he like to sing? How does he feel about his life? What's important to him in this world—and what's not important? What would *he* like to talk about?"

The woman said she didn't really know, because the alcoholism had long been the central issue for her. "For a long time," she said, "I've just been waiting for my parents to sort of get their life together, to have some sort of happiness. I've always felt that I was a burden—that everything around them was a burden. So I just want them to rid themselves of these problems. I know he's going to die soon. If the alcohol doesn't kill him, his heart's going to give out—or something."

"You're probably right," I said. "And if he's going to die soon, that means your time together is limited. Perhaps you can't control his drinking, but his drinking is not your responsibility. Your happiness is. When you can take more responsibility for your own life and less responsibility for his, then you can have a different conversation with him. Talk to him about your life, about your relationship with him. You can tell him about your tender feelings. But please, don't try to control him. It's disrespectful to both of you."

The daughter must have known she would never "cure" her father of alcoholism. When she went into therapy, she was admitting her defeat. Yet she was still looking for a way to win.

Both for alcoholics and for children of alcoholics, no change can begin to happen until they admit defeat. The first step in Alcoholics Anonymous is to say, "We are powerless over alcohol." But it's also important to admit that we're powerless over the alcoholic. Once we acknowledge our powerlessness, we can start to regain some control over our own lives.

In alcoholic families, as in so many other families, we just don't know each other. We create images of each other. The adult daughter of an alcoholic creates an image of her father, and he creates an image of her and of himself. They relate to the images. They don't get to know each other, and they don't get to *feel* known.

"I don't think it's too late," I told the thirty-year-old woman with a seventy-year-old, addicted parent. "I think you still have the opportunity to feel known in your family. And I think the more of you that you share, the more known you will feel. I'm not talking about telling *him* about *him*. I mean telling *him* about *you*."

"I've always been afraid to do that," she said.

"Yes. It's very frightening."

On Glenn's first visit to my office, he described symptoms that are typical of the adult child of an alcoholic. A thirty-four-year-old man with a ten-year-old son of his own, Glenn felt inadequate. He did not trust his sense of reality, because of the denial and distortions in his own family. At the same time, Glenn was enraged at his father and he blamed his father for all the problems in his life.

Glenn's father had done some terrible things to the boy when he was a child. There had been acts of omission as well as acts of commission. And Glenn had carried the rage against his father for all these years. Now Glenn wanted to be close to his own son in a way that his father had never been close to him.

One day in therapy, Glenn told me he had just seen the movie *Field of Dreams*. There was a lot of sadness in his voice as he told me how the son in the movie finally plays a game of catch with his father. This was something Glenn had dreamed of all his life. He realized how much he *still* longed to have that game of catch with his father.

For Glenn, this was impossible. His father was now in his mid-seventies, and he was still drinking. Glenn would never play catch with his father—he knew it, and he was filled with rage at the father who had never been there for him.

I had hoped Glenn would be able to look beyond his rage, which was something he was eventually able to do in the context of our relationship. When he was with me, he was again with a man who could not play catch with him—but a man who cared about him and was interested in what was going on inside him.

At one point he said, "I hate what happened to you. I hate what you have to live with."

But I think what he hated was what he and I *couldn't have* in our relationship. So I talked to him about how I, too, hated what had happened to me and how much I would have loved to play catch with him.

His eyes welled with tears when he said, "I would love that, too, for both our sakes."

And my eyes also filled with tears.

Once he was able to get in touch with those more painful and tender feelings, Glenn could express the longing for more contact with his father and his sense of hurt for not having that contact. Glenn began to feel those honest feelings instead of feeling defeat, feeling like a victim. He realized that he longed for contact—longed to play ball. He knew that even though his father wasn't available, he had options in his life.

Gradually, Glenn's relationship with his own son began to change. He was able to play catch with his son. He started to collect baseball cards and coach Little League.

And something else happened: he developed a different kind of relationship with his own father. That relationship was not as intimate and loving as he would have liked, but it was certainly a lot closer than it had been before he expressed the grief that was part of his rage. That game of catch would never happen, but even so, he could be close to his father in a way that he had not been before.

5
_____

How Can They Let Go of Us—
and How Can We Let Go of Them?

ॐ

A dear friend of mine at the radio station told me a story about having lunch with her father, a doctor in his mid-sixties.

Her father has practiced medicine in Philadelphia for more than thirty years. During lunch, he talked about some of his experiences, and then—since they were near the hospital where he had worked—father and daughter strolled over to the medical building to look at a plaque on the wall. Her father showed her where her grandfather's name was engraved. She watched the pride in his face while he spoke.

Then they walked back to the train station. On the way to the station, he told her a funny story. She recalled that he stopped on the street corner to deliver the punch line.

They laughed.

He turned to go.

And as she was watching him walk toward the station, my friend thought, "Oh, God, please don't let anything happen to him!"

And then it occurred to her that, all these years, as she took off for school, for summer camp, for college—for all her madcap adventures—he had been saying just the same thing: "Oh, God, please don't let anything happen to her."

In time, children begin to be aware of feeling the protectiveness and fear that their parents carry. As we grow up and leave, our parents feel protective toward us. They hope, or pray, that we'll come to no harm. But that wish goes two ways. And as they struggle with how-to-let-go-of-us, we struggle with how-to-let-go-of-them.

Emotionally, "letting go" is synonymous with concepts like separation, abandonment, and loneliness. That's what makes letting go so painful and frightening, and I believe that's why we often try to avoid it. What we are really avoiding are the anxiety and fright that come with separation.

As often happens during our parents' crises, we may try to avoid these painful emotions by trying to control our parents or by telling them how to behave. If we're informing them how often they should go to doctors, and which ones they should see, we're avoiding our pain and fear. Our parents, on the other hand, may be avoiding similar emotions by telling us how to raise our children and manage our lives.

Instinctively, we learn how to separate from our parents. But if they haven't taught us well, it becomes our responsibility to teach them. And perhaps not enough of us have the same kind of courage to deal with our anxiety and aloneness that my colleague and her father had.

"I'm eighty years old and I have two children, forty and forty-two." The caller's voice was strong and clear. "The children really aren't very demonstrative or very communicative. Sometimes, you know," here the woman laughed, "I wonder if they think I'm already dead. But I have really felt that they're *afraid* of my death. I'm doing very well, and yet I feel I have to prepare them in some way to get along without me."

I asked what she would like her children to do differently if she were able to change them.

"I'd like them to be more affectionate," she said. "I think they have my interests at heart, but I need their affection. I guess I've always been so independent that they don't think of me as a needy person."

As the woman was speaking, I tried to imagine how her children were receiving her message of neediness. How were they to know this woman was needy if she concealed her feelings behind a veil of independence? What roundabout means did she use to communicate with them?

Perhaps she lavished gifts—hoping that their appreciation in return would express the affection and caring that she needed. Perhaps she continually invited them to visit—incompletely stifling her disappointment each time they declined. Perhaps she called frequently—"keeping up" with their lives while telling them little about herself. Or perhaps she withdrew from them—leading her own life and keeping them guessing about where she was and what she was doing.

Like all of us, this woman held somewhere in her mind the image of what her relationship with her children *should* be at this stage of her life. But her children weren't living up to that image. She didn't really know what they thought of her or whether they understood *anything* about her. In fact, she wondered whether she had already "died" for them.

So the eighty-year-old woman was "protecting" her children from her fears, her dependence, her death, her hurt. But what she was really "protecting" them from was her heart.

—◊◊◊—

But there's a problem with protectiveness.

On one occasion I was fortunate to have dinner with the late noted psychologist and author Bruno Bettelheim, when he was a guest speaker at the annual conference of the Family Institute of Philadelphia. The conversation was all I could have wished—rich with references to the work that interested both of us at the time—and we were in agreement on many topics. But, as always, it was what we *disagreed* about that I would remember most distinctly:

"One of the cardinal rules in all relationships," he said, "is to never hurt the other person if it can possibly be avoided."

He was talking about marriage relationships—but I immediately thought of intergenerational family relationships in which people were taking great pains "not to hurt the other person."

"Are you suggesting we should wear kid gloves with each other?" I asked.

"Yes," he said.

"Well, that's kind. But when we wear kid gloves with each other, we can never feel each other's flesh."

I think that's what the eighty-year-old woman was complaining about—that she couldn't feel her children's flesh.

What if we "feel" our parents' trying to hold on to us? We may be feeling their need to control or their intrusiveness. But what's really going on inside them is their fear of loss, of abandonment, of alienation. That fear is rarely expressed directly. Instead, it's expressed in the code that parents and children often use to mask their emotions from each other.

Sylvia, a retired professional woman who was a grandmother, told me about her son Martin and his wife Amy who had moved to Houston with their two children. Since her retirement,

Sylvia had been putting a great deal of energy into volunteer work for the Institute of the Blind. She had organized a traveling exhibit that would be going to Houston.

Sylvia had sent her son and daughter-in-law advance notice that the exhibit was coming. She had secretly wished that her grandchildren would see the exhibit. After all, it was something she was proud of and she hoped her grandchildren, too, would be proud of it. But though the exhibit had been in Houston for two months, her son's family had not seen it.

Now she was hurt, angry, confused. Why didn't they understand how important it all was to her? Were they *deliberately* trying to hurt her feelings?

I wondered whether Sylvia had been able to tell Martin and Amy about her neediness, as she was now telling me. Often, when we are ashamed of our own needs, we don't express them. We hope that someone will pick up on them or deduce them and then meet those needs without asking. *Then* we would be happy. But even if people are paying a lot of attention, if they have to guess what we're thinking, they'll only be right about fifty percent of the time—if that!

For Sylvia's message to be heard, she would have to take the risk of saying to her son and daughter-in-law, "I have some needs—whether you can meet them or not. In the same way you needed me to be proud of you as a child, I need you to be proud of me.

"Martin and Amy, I need your involvement in my life, because I love you and I'd like you to love me in the same way. And at the age I am, I'm a little insecure and a little lonely."

It would be a risk for Sylvia to say those words. Possibly, her son would respond, "No—I can't help you with your needs or make you feel less lonely."

But if you could put yourself in Martin's place, if Sylvia were your mother, how would it feel to listen to her say, "I need you to love me—I'm feeling insecure and lonely."

Does this feel intrusive or oppressive?

And then consider how you would feel if she tried to hide her neediness and, instead, asked, "Why don't you come to my show? I'm sure you can spare just a couple of hours to see my show!" That's less risky for her—but surely feels more oppressive to the son.

The more vulnerable we make ourselves, the more available we become to be heard and to be touched. If Sylvia could say what she was feeling in her heart, perhaps Martin and Amy would be able to answer her needs directly. It would be Sylvia's risk, of course—but that risk would give her a chance to be truly heard.

Perhaps there are different degrees of letting go. At one extreme is the refusal to let go—the daily phone calls, the control, the mutual intrusiveness and resentment—*not* letting go as a way of not feeling the anxiety and fear. At the other extreme is the loving daughter who, watching her father cross the street, gives up control and says to herself, "Oh, God, I hope nothing happens to him."

There is a wealth of generosity in the second kind of letting go. Whether or not we ask a higher power to help with the looking-after, simply to say, "I *hope* nothing happens to this person" is a loving statement. It is a statement that expresses the courage to give up the myth of control.

When we give up the myth that we can control our parents, perhaps then we can give up the fear of their controlling us.

Perhaps then we can take off the kid gloves and touch each other, without fear that we'll be glued to each other's need and pain. We'll never figure out how to stop each other from being needy or hurting; all we can really do is figure out what to say inside ourselves as we let go of each other.

6

How Can We Feel Safe with Them?

At some time in our lives, parents seem all-powerful. Their words or actions can hurt us deeply. What they say about us can also wound deeply—a grudging, a slighting, or a demeaning remark can make us fear them or make us ashamed of ourselves. Ideally, as we grow older, the feelings of harshness and/or disappointment are usually softened by a greater understanding of who they were and who we were "back then" when we were children—and also a clearer appreciation of why we felt wronged, shamed, or abandoned. Even so, we may continue to feel unsafe when we're near them, as if we were still children who could be wounded again, as we were earlier.

Sometimes a grown child's fears are so strong that they hold an almost mythic power over him. Like a character of mythology, whose graven image remains unchanged through the ages, a parent's image may remain engraved in a person's consciousness in a shape that refuses to change as the years go by.

The story that I'm about to tell—tragic in its dimensions—is about the power of that kind of myth. For, at their most powerful, these myths that we carry can make us feel unsafe for the rest of our lives.

Hillary was a thin, gray-haired woman in her mid-fifties when she and her husband Craig began seeing me. She had grown up on a farm in northern New Jersey; she and Craig now lived in Camden. They had first met at a church group meeting when Hillary was working as a secretary and Craig was getting his master's degree in business administration. Married when Hillary was twenty and Craig was twenty-four, they were childless.

It would be hard to imagine anyone more easygoing or less offensive than Craig. Balding, pleasant, he had a cherubic presence—often smiling, sometimes joking. Having settled comfortably into a middle-management position, he devoted considerable energy to hobbies and community work. Boy Scouts and Rotary Club were high on his list. He was a deacon in his church. As he cited all the male-oriented activities in which he was involved, it became apparent to me that he and Hillary could not be spending a lot of time together.

Hillary had been the one to call me, complaining of "distance" from her husband. They agreed that the distance had existed for years—almost the life of the marriage. They did not talk easily about their sex life. Craig sobered at first mention of the subject. Early in their marriage they had had some intimacy, but Hillary said she "didn't want to go on" after she realized they couldn't have children. When I asked whether there were medical reasons for not having children, Hillary said, "Craig's count was low." Finding little or no pleasure in sex, Hillary had willingly extricated herself from what she called "lovemaking" soon after the report of "Craig's condition."

With all the warmth and geniality that Craig exuded, he obviously had affection to spare. But since his wife had kept her distance emotionally as well as sexually, he had poured his energy into all those other "safe" activities that he had listed. Yet Hillary said she wanted to be closer to him. She could list his appealing qualities with true appreciation, and she said he was "very kind."

What emerged was a portrait of two people living side-by-side, parallel lives, always with distance between them, rarely touching emotionally or physically: two people who now wanted closeness—and didn't know how to get it.

There were two figures in Hillary's family background whom I wanted to know more about. One was a sister two years older who had "disappeared" when Hillary was eleven. That sister had "run away from home," and Hillary had never seen her again. The other was her father.

Though Hillary's mother had died before she reached her teens, her father was still living. He was eighty years old, had emphysema, and was living in a nursing home. Hillary went to see him once a week.

"Your father raised you and your sister?" I asked.

"My sister ran away," she reminded me.

"Why?"

"I don't know," said Hillary. "She just got sick of him, I guess."

"Did you get sick of him?"

"No, he never bothered me," she replied.

Later we returned to the subject—in a different context. We were talking about Craig and Hillary's difficulty with intimacy when I asked Hillary to talk about her relationship with another male, her father. I explained that the emotional patterns that we develop in our family of origin are often repeated in the relationship that we later have with our spouse.

When Hillary talked about her father, she was visibly distressed. She squirmed in her seat and broke eye contact with me for the first time in the session. She seemed annoyed, even angry, that we had to pursue this subject.

I asked her whether she was uncomfortable, and she said, "Yes."

Months later, we returned to the subject. By now, our relationship was deeper and therapy was safer. Hillary said she was closer to her father now than she had ever been, but she added that she really didn't like him. Again she was evasive, though not nearly as evasive as previously.

At the following session, she was visibly upset when she came in. She said she needed to talk. I waited—giving her all the room she needed. She stared at the floor for at least three minutes, struggling to find the words and the courage to tell her story.

With difficulty, she told me what had happened.

When Hillary was eleven, she had come upon her father and her sister having sex in the barn behind the house. It appeared to be a rape.

When Hillary's father came out of the barn, he told her, "If you ever tell anyone what you saw, I'll kill you."

Later the same night, Hillary's sister said to her, "He'll never do that to me again."

The sister left home the next day. Hillary had not heard from her since.

For over forty years, my patient had lived in terror that she would be killed by her father. She had never talked about it—never admitted it, even to her husband. She had continued to obey her father's injunction that she never tell anyone. And for more than forty years she had remained petrified of him.

I asked her to bring in a recent picture of her father. She did.

"That's the man you're frightened of," I said.

Of course, the fifty-five-year-old woman knew she didn't have to be afraid of an eighty-year-old man. It was the *eleven*-year-old girl inside her who was frightened.

Hillary had to feel secure that her father wouldn't or couldn't kill her. The sense of security didn't happen magically. As well as getting in touch with her sense of fear, she had to get in touch with her sense of rage and her sense of violation. When she "owned" those feelings, instead of removing herself from them, she became more powerful Once she discovered that she didn't have to hide from her own feelings of rage, her father "magically" became more real and therefore less frightening.

Hillary's experience was extreme. Not many of us live in such terror of a parent. Yet each of us in our own way must deal with our parents' pseudo-mythic powers. They are giants in our early lives. If we have ever felt unsafe in their presence, that feeling does not miraculously vanish—though their power dwindles as we grow up and grow away from them.

Perhaps a son heard his father call him "a klutz" for dropping the football. Does it surprise you that the grown-up son still feels like a klutz whenever he's with his father?

Perhaps, during her teenage years, a girl's mother was always trying to get her to lose weight. Now the grown-up daughter is a mature woman, comfortable with herself and her appearance—*except* when she spends time with her mother. Those times, she feels criticized and unattractive.

The son who got all A's in high school remembers his mother's almost-panicked anxiety when he dropped out of college for a year. Today that young man, a successful professional, feels his mother is questioning his reliability every time she asks about his family or his practice.

A daughter who came in second in the regional skating championships will never forget the anger in her father's face when he said, "You *almost* won—God damn it." Today, the thirty-five-year-old bank vice president knows perfectly well why she feels so inadequate whenever she's around her father. But she says she can't stop herself from feeling that way.

We don't *want* to feel unsafe with them. And the voice of reason tells us that we *shouldn't* feel that way.

But what does reason have to do with it? We're dealing with figures who, to children, are giants. And these people remain giants to the child within us. We're wrestling with mythic powers that refuse to be doubted out of existence.

And the feeling of safety must come from within.

My patient had to feel secure that her father wouldn't or couldn't kill her. She had to get in touch with her own power, so that her father would become less frightening.

Hillary's husband was present at the session when she talked about her father, but for the next few sessions she wanted to be alone. Her feelings so overwhelmed her that she didn't even trust having her husband in the room while she was talking about them. Hillary's fear of her father, and her hatred of him, consumed her. She wept—she wished him dead. She actually thought about killing him. The most destructive feeling she struggled with was her guilt about her sister. She felt responsible, and she had a terrible, terrible sense of shame. She hated herself for not having done anything.

In time, Hillary was able to tell her husband. They cried together—and talked about the fury they felt.

As a result of opening up to her family, Hillary discovered that she was still lovable to them. Even though she was never able to forgive her father, she was able to forgive herself. The others took her lead, and gradually the fury at her father, shared by every member of the family, was dissipated. And Hillary's father became more real to her.

Eventually, Hillary went to the nursing home and talked to her father about his future and about what he wanted. She never talked about what happened forty-odd years ago. She never fully forgave him; she still carries some of the burden of that fateful day. But she got to know him better than she ever had. And the mythic power he had wielded over her—the power to destroy—has all but vanished.

How can we get the echo of parental voices out of our heads, unless we replace them with real voices—the voices of parents who (now that we are adults) have diminished power over our lives? Think what power the "klutz" would have if he could say to his father, "Dad, remember that time I dropped the football in that big game . . . ?" Could the grown-up daughter joke with her mother about her high-school days, when she always felt over-weight? If the "drop-out" son could ask his mother about the panic she felt when he "took off" for a year—wouldn't her questions seem less like "prying" to him?

My guess is that each of us feels safer when we touch the moment and rob it of its mythic power. Perhaps we can never truly see our parents as they really are. Perhaps we will still feel some pain, fear, or anger in their presence. But on the other hand, we may be able to reduce that element of distortion and pause for a moment to discover that it is not our parents we fear—it's our own history.

And safety may be very near at hand.

7

How Can We Make It Safe *for* Them?

∾

For about a year, I had been treating John, a lawyer in his mid-thirties. One of the issues that "had him stuck" was his feelings about his father. John was angry with his father because he thought his father never heard him, never acknowledged him, never respected him. And at the same time he was protective of his father; he felt his father was fragile, so he held his anger in and never expressed it.

Here was a man who was a terrific success in every regard. John was already a partner in a well-established firm. He was a warm, bright, sensitive, and very likable young man. Yet he carried bitterness, anger, and hurt—all tied in to his relationship with his father.

John told me that he had felt quite intimate with his father until he was nine years old. When he was nine, his father, a real-estate agent, got into financial difficulty on a large commercial venture; he was indicted on a forgery charge and lost his license. As a result, the family plunged into near-bankruptcy. All the family relationships broke up—everyone grew much more distant.

My patient had never talked about this episode to anyone else in his family. It was never brought up. The issues were too painful. I encouraged John to invite his father to therapy.

John's father was a large, balding man who wore a dark business suit to this meeting with his son. Unlike John, who was understandably quite comfortable in the therapeutic setting—this was, after all, his "territory"—his father looked at the living-room-style surroundings of my office as if they were unsuitable for a professional person. He avoided looking directly either at me or at his son. Although there was a comfortable sofa, he chose to take a seat in the one straight-backed chair in the room.

I guided the session, but I left it to John to ask the questions. After some time, John said to his father, "Dad, I feel like there's a barrier between us. Our relationship is important to me and I want to bring that barrier down."

John's father nodded.

His son continued, "Dad, I feel you've never really understood me. But at the same time, I've never really understood you."

For the next five minutes, John fumbled around for the right words to say. Finally, out of frustration, I intervened for him: "Dad," I said, speaking for John, "tell me what happened when you lost your license and had to stop real-estate work."

John's father began to tell, very matter-of-factly, what had happened.

I asked him how he felt about it. With a great deal of difficulty, he began to talk about his hurt, minimizing it all the while. As gently as possible, I interrupted, saying, "How often do you think about it? The reason I ask," I went on, "is that every time I think about the days when I used to walk, it causes a searing pain inside."

His reply was, "There's not a day goes by that I don't think about it. I would give up everything and take a menial job if it could afford me the chance to do what I used to do in life."

John wept quietly as he heard this.

At the end of the session, I thanked the father for his openness and his trust in both of us.

My patient never did get a chance to tell his father who he was and what he was about. He didn't feel he was heard by his father. But he got something far more important: That wall came down. He was able to touch his father and feel touched by him for the first time in twenty-five years.

None of us can truly hear each other when we carry burdens of shame, guilt, and embarrassment. And those were the feelings that John's father carried with him every day. He felt ashamed of himself and guilty about the shame he thought he'd caused his family. He'd been punishing himself for the last twenty-five years by keeping this distance.

John was angry at his father and he was hurt about the loss of intimacy. Perhaps John was angry because he felt entitled to be understood—or perhaps he was angry at the deprivation and loss. All of his anger was understandable. His job, however, was to reach out to his father. Otherwise, John would never have been able to touch the father he once had.

For me, there is an association between John's experience in his own life and what happened between my friends and me after my accident. Some people were frightened—frightened of what was going on inside me and them. Some of the people who stayed away from me, I just decided to hate. And I still do.

But some of these relationships were important to me. And as hurt, physically and emotionally, as I was, I had to reach out and hold their hands and tell them it was okay to be with me. When I did that, I was fraught with ambivalence: I felt, *"I'm* suffing and *I'm* needy—why should *I* be the one to reach out?" On the other hand, *not* to reach out would mean the end of the relationship.

What would it mean to *not* reach out to our parents? I guess the issue is simple. After all, we can't just "write off" our parents—they live inside us. I think it's our responsibility to acknowledge them and their feelings. Parents may feel helpless, vulnerable, confused, out of control, angry, disappointed—but parents do *feel*. The best way we can make it safe for them is just to be aware of that. And when we talk to them, we can wonder aloud what they're feeling.

When children are very young, they don't have to take care of their parents; they can expect their parents to take care of them. But once we're past a certain age—when we're thirty, forty, or fifty—it's we who must hear our parents. It's we who must nurture them. It's we who must respect their dignity and integrity.

I think that's what we need to carry into the so-called confrontation. And so my recommendation is that if you want to be heard, you must listen very carefully and then speak your part. But make sure you do it in that order.

8

What Do We Expect of Our Parents?

∽

I'm going to tell two stories. the first concerns two girls, ages three and four—and their father, who they thought was a superman. The second is about a forty-year-old man and his father, an avid golfer.

Unlikely as it may seem, I think these stories address the same theme.

The girls are my own daughters. When Debbie was three and Ali was four, we went on a long family trip in the car. The girls were in back in their car seats; my wife Sandy and I were in front. About halfway to our destination, the car slowed and we heard a flapping sound that Sandy identified instantly.

"Oh, no, we've got a flat tire."

I pulled over to the side of the road. Sandy and I were dismayed—what a way to start a vacation! With dread, I faced the prospect of unloading a fully packed trunk to get at the spare and changing a tire on the noisy, dusty highway. Lunchtime was approaching, and the girls would soon be hungry. The whole situation was enough to discourage anyone.

Then a voice piped up from the backseat.

"Don't worry," said Ali. "Daddy will 'crix' it. He'll just pick up the car—and he'll 'crix' it."

And there I was—Daddy the superman, with the strength of millions, capable of "crixing" tires in a single stroke.

The other perspective comes from forty-year-old Kevin, a man who was telling me about his retired father and how he played far too much golf for his own good. Kevin said his father had recently retired to Florida and was now spending nearly all his time on the golf course. From Kevin's point of view, his father's "compulsion" had gotten out of hand. Kevin said his father wasn't spending enough time with his wife. Even when his children and grandchildren visited, he spent more time on the golf course than he spent with his family.

"Is there a problem with that?" I asked.

"Well, he doesn't communicate well," Kevin replied. "He isolates himself. It builds a wall around him—it's hard to describe, but it's there. And if I try to penetrate that wall, there's anger."

Kevin went on to say how much pain he felt at not having access to his father, not seeing him as much as he would like, and not being able to talk to him. And as I listened, I wondered whether there was a connection between forty-year-old Kevin and my four-year-old daughter. Both were children with expectations—the often-unrealistic expectations that all of us have of our parents. Ali saw her father as a superman, someone who could just pick up the car and fix the tire. At some point, sad to say, she would have to give up that image of him.

At forty, Kevin expected his father to be someone who was nurturing, a close friend, and confidant, a father who *should* be more concerned about making his son feel good than playing golf. Kevin would have to let go of the image of a nurturing father—ideally, give up all of his expectations of his father. And then he could relate to the man as he is.

Of course, for Kevin to give up that image would involve a loss—and I knew from an experience with my own father how painful such a loss could be.

For years, I played frequent games of golf with my father, and he always beat me. Even when I got much better at the game, he always managed to win by a significant margin.

One evening, my wife Sandy and I went out to dinner with my parents and with my sister and brother-in-law. At the end of the meal, we had the usual dispute over who would pay the bill. Always, in the past, my father had won the argument and picked up the tab. But this particular evening, my brother-in-law ended up paying for dinner.

As we were sitting at the table having coffee after the meal, I looked across at my father, and suddenly, for the first time, I saw how old he was. I saw the wrinkles in his forehead and hands; his cheeks looked saggy, and his eyes were tired. I felt very loving, but I also felt very sad. I realized that my father couldn't "crix" things for me anymore.

The next day, I beat my father at golf for the first time. But there was no thrill in the victory. I felt a little pride—but mostly sadness. The ideal father was not quite as strong and sure as he used to be.

Whenever we lose the ideal, perfect parent that we carry around in our heads, we lose a measure of shelter and safety. Without the image of a parent going ahead of us into the world, we feel ourselves—perhaps for the first time—traveling solo through uncharted territory.

What happens when the four-year-old grows up to discover that her father *can't* fix everything? What will happen to Kevin when he finally gives up trying to get the kind of companionship and nurture that he wants from his father?

How does any of us feel when he stops looking to his parents for something that they cannot provide?

Not only did Ali have a distorted image of me; I was, to her, the *perfect* father. So the four-year-old expected *everything* of me. And how did she feel when she didn't get it?

How did you feel the first time you didn't get what you wanted from a parent?

Angry? Hurt? Scared?

Some of our childish needs don't change a lot when we're older. We expect non-nurturing parents to be nurturing—and we're angry when they're not. We expect depressed parents *not* to be depressed. We expect parents who have a bad marriage to make it better, so we can feel safer and so they can feel better about themselves.

And one thing we don't expect is for our parents to grow older—although we know it's going to happen. As long as they're alive, we expect them to be the all-powerful parents who will always, somehow, recognize our needs and be there for us.

The first day of my accident when I was in the intensive care unit of Ephrata Hospital, I woke up and saw my parents standing near with their worried faces, staring down at me. And I realized that they had no idea what I was feeling, what I was experiencing, or what my future looked like.

I realized that for all of my life, I had assumed they were pathfinders for me. Anyplace I was about to go, they had been before. I had an image of all-powerful parents having the knowledge that I needed. But when I woke up that morning and saw them, I realized at that moment they were no longer my pathfinders. I was about to go off on my own path.

I think this is common to all of us. I think we all go off on our own path. But our assumptions about our parents often stay with us.

Not all of our expectations are related to making our parents more wonderful than they really are. We may also expect to be disappointed by our parents. And when we take that disappointment into new relationships, we often find ways of confirming it.

Ruth, a fifty-year-old woman, is married to Ed, a small-town lawyer. He makes a nice living, but not nice enough for her. He isn't smart enough for her. She has not gained the status or social prestige that she wanted when she went into the marriage. Her daughter, Sandra, grew up feeling close to her mother; she saw her father through her mother's eyes. So she was equally disappointed in him. He wasn't smart enough, important enough, or successful enough for the daughter, either. She secretly craved intimacy and closeness with her father but couldn't seek either with him, out of loyalty to her mother. The father, of course, played a role in this, too. He was depressed, and he accepted his wife and daughter's criticism.

Sandra, the daughter who is now thirty-one, grew up expecting to be disappointed in her mate. She faces the same dilemma with her husband-to-be, David, that she had with her father: she expects intimacy with him but can't acknowledge it, can't express it because of loyalty to her mother. She never asks what goes on inside him, and she never tells him what goes on inside her. Though she has already concluded that David will disappoint her in some ways, she says she is quite certain that this is the man she wants to marry. Essentially, her family of origin has already prepared her to expect disappointment as a "given" in any marriage.

How do we give up the expectations that we have of our parents? We have to bury the illusion of what a parent *should* be or *could* be.

"Find the perfect mother in your head—" I urged Nancy, a young single woman who was still struggling to get attention and nurture from her mom. "Imagine every detail of the *perfect* woman—the woman you would like to have as your mother. Imagine how she dresses, how she talks to you, to your dad, to your sister and brothers. Imagine her smile and her touch. What does it feel like when this mother puts her arms around you and hugs you? Imagine that she is giving you all the love and support you ever wanted from a mother.

"And now," I said, "say your last words to her. Say good-bye to her and take her inside you—so that imaginary woman is inside of you, and the real mother is now outside.

"Your real mother is still alive. She may be imperfect and selfish—but you might as well accept her, because you'll never have the imaginary mom who's inside your head, no matter how hard you reach out to find her."

A few weeks later, Nancy's mother came with her daughter to see me.

And afterward, Nancy said: "You know what? I think if there was a Handicapped Olympics for mothers, *my* mother would be a medalist."

The parent in Nancy's head had to die before she could admire the "Olympic medalist" qualities of the real woman who was her real mother—with all her limitations, handicaps, and flaws. The imaginary mother had to be buried—solemnly, privately, with respect—but buried all the same, before Nancy could have a mother who was just her real mother, and nothing more.

9

Learning Our Parents' Losses

∾

A colleague whose mother was dying said to me with tears in her eyes, "I never realized how my mother lived inside my very core." So, as her mother dies, she's losing her mother and she's losing something inside her.

How, then, do we separate our parents' losses from our own losses? What do their losses *mean* to us? Is there a *need* to winnow theirs from ours?

As our parents age, their losses become more apparent to us, and we may be tempted to feel that we can understand those losses or that we can fix things for them. But as our parents become weaker or sicker or less capable of caring for themselves, our attempts to do things for them, however well-meaning, may erode their dignity in more ways than we realize.

When our dignity is intact, others listen to us, respect our privacy, and ask us what we want before they take steps to care for us. Too often, when we have losses, these are precisely the privileges that we lose. After my accident, I experienced the feeling of being helplessly immobilized in a hospital bed. Doctors and nurses came and went without asking permission to enter or leave my room. They would come in at any time of the day or night, examine my naked body, leave me uncovered, and leave the door open.

I didn't care. I had lost my sense of dignity.

Then, one night at about ten o'clock, a nurse asked whether she could talk to me. She told me she was suicidal. We talked for about two hours. I had to reach into myself, to draw on my resources as a professional, as a parent, as a human being. She was not at my bedside as a caregiver; she simply needed someone to talk to that night.

After she left, I slept through until morning. It was the first time that had happened since I was admitted to the hospital. I realized that, for all my losses, I still had dignity and worth. And for the next six months of my hospitalization, I battled the doctors and nurses who tried to take my dignity away from me. When they left me uncovered, I asked them to please fix the sheets. When they left the door open, I asked them to close it. When they entered without knocking, I reminded them that this was my room. One doctor in particular used to raise his voice a few decibels every time he talked to me. Perhaps he was unaware of it, but I clearly heard the change in his voice. It offended me, and I confronted him with it, reminding him there was nothing wrong with my hearing.

Later, I felt that my dignity was safe from such violations. I could still feel insulted, but those insults do not compromise my dignity. I no longer have to do battle: my dignity is within me and it can't be taken away.

My uncle Irv, who had always been a very independent man, was dying of lung cancer. Though he was in the final stages, his family, understandably, didn't want him to die. Of course, the family couldn't be passive about his illness, so they were taking him to various hospitals for therapy and diagnoses.

During this period, I went to visit him at his home. The man was terribly debilitated, both from the cancer and from the treatment. He said to me, "Danny, what do I do if they want to put me in the hospital again and give me more chemotherapy?"

And I said, "Irv, in spite of all of your losses, the one thing you still have is your dignity. Do what you need to do to maintain your dignity."

He cried and said, "Thank you."

In my heart I know that he did die with his dignity. And I also feel that I gave him a small gift—a token of appreciation for everything he'd given me throughout his life.

One thing that happens as we get older and experience loss is that we begin to feel worthless. When we lose our stamina, our ability to walk, our independence, we feel there is less of us there, and therefore we are *worth less.* And if our losses affect our independence, we feel like a burden.

The night the nurse came and talked to me for two hours, talked because *she* needed *me,* I was fortunate. Someone helped me realize that I did have value and was not a burden. In the months that followed, as a result of my disability, I certainly demanded a lot from my family both physically and emotionally. But I was beginning to realize I was able to give something back in terms of parenting, child rearing, giving affection to my wife, and making contributions to my profession.

I think we all have something to give back. And it's very important for us all to be aware of what we have of value. If our parents have suffered losses, and feel worthless and burdensome, we can help them understand what they have to give.

We can help them keep their lives in balance. What happens when we become older or lose some function is that we *take* more than we *give*. That puts our lives out of balance, and that's part of what makes us depressed.

It's important to have both the give and the take. If we respect the dignity of a parent who has endured a loss, we can have the courage to climb into that parent's world for a moment and ask what it's like. What's it like to be retired? To be seventy, eighty, or ninety? What's it like to be alcoholic? Or angry? Or ill and in pain? What's it like to be put into the hospital or moved into a nursing home? What do these things feel like?

To ask is a dignified human interaction. Everything that comes after is secondary.

Anne, a young woman with a family, had willingly taken her aging grandfather into her home. As a girl, she had been very close to her grandfather, and she had looked forward to having him in her house again. But after he moved in, Anne found that he often complained about feeling like a burden to the family. Living in his own home, he had been active and had maintained many close friendships. But after he moved in with Anne and her family, he went out less often, communicated less with friends, and had fewer activities.

Finally Anne sought counseling. The counselor recommended that she get her grandfather more involved with activities in the senior center and suggested various ways that the grandfather could sustain a feeling of usefulness in the family. But when the granddaughter took this advice home and tried it with her grandfather, he showed little interest in changing his ways.

She now felt as if she had tried everything. What else could she do?

"Your grandfather has experienced a whole lot of losses," I said to her. "And encouraging him to do things he doesn't want to do represents another kind of loss for him—perhaps, in a way, a loss of self-control, maybe even dignity."

It seemed to me there was something central to her grandfather's sense of himself—and his dignity—that Anne was unlikely to change. I told her about a workshop on aging that I had attended the previous year. At the workshop I met two elderly men, both of whom had led active professional lives in the mental health field. Someone at the workshop asked both of them: "How do you deal with death? How do you deal with dying?"

The first man said, "I'm very upset about how close I am to death. I hate it. There are so many things in life to do that I'll never get to do now. And I just don't like it. It's with me all the time."

The other man said, "Well, I don't think about it much. I'm much too busy, and I'm having a good time."

I think these two men just had different character structures. The same things were available to both of them. They just had different personalities, and neither of them could change.

I wondered aloud whether this was the "problem" Anne's grandfather had. And perhaps she should ask him what he wanted—find out what his needs were in this stage in his life.

It's important that we respect the way our parents want to deal with their losses, that we find out what their losses are, and then find out how they feel about them. Some parents want to talk about them, even though they are afraid. Some just *don't* want to talk about them—and never have, their whole lives.

We all learned how to deal with our losses from our family of origin. Our parents have lost their parents. And we learned about grieving through the way they grieved. I don't think it's fair to our parents if we go out and learn new ways of dealing with losses—ways that work better for us—and then try to impose those ways on our parents.

As our parents' losses grow, we may discover how much they still can share with us. We can respect their dignity enough to ask them what their needs are. And when we have needs of our own, we can acknowledge their dignity by asking whether they will listen.

10

Making Peace with Our Parents

ॐ

It's hard to imagine that a grown woman could hate the act of making tea for her mother—but so it was.

When Marianne was six years old and had just started school, she learned the pattern that was to be repeated throughout her school years. As soon as she got off the bus and walked into her house, she heard her mother's voice.

"Marianne, is that you?"

"Yes, Mom."

"I'm so glad you're home." Marianne waited for the next line, which was always the same: "Marianne, dear, I've got a terrible headache. Would you mind making your mother a cup of tea?"

Repeated, day after day.

To the six-year-old, nothing would have seemed out of the ordinary if all her friends made tea for *their* mothers when they got home from school. But a child quickly learns what school-mates are doing. Marianne discovered that most of her friends' mothers made snacks for their children when they came home. *Other* mothers made plans for their daughters to meet friends, or take piano lessons, or go to the playground. Marianne could see that her mother was different from the others. She wasn't making plans and looking out for her daughter; instead, she was asking her daughter to look out for *her*.

Marianne boiled the water. She poured the tea, made up a tray, and took it into the living room. Her mother, resting in a big armchair, smiled as Marianne came into the room. Marianne always poured the tea carefully. She put in just the right amount of milk and sugar, stirred the tea, and handed the cup to her mother without spilling a drop.

"Thank you, Marianne. I'm so glad you came home—just in time. I hope you had a nice day at school. Would you like to get a snack for yourself?"

Yes, of course, she wanted a snack for herself. But she didn't want to *get* it for herself. She wanted the kind of mother who fixed a snack *for her*. And no matter how often or how keenly she wished for that miracle to happen, it never did.

And it never would, in all the years she was growing up.

"My mother always needed someone to look after her," Marianne observed, three decades later. "If it wasn't me, it was my father. She didn't know how to be a mother."

Another patient tells me, "My mother was overprotective. She wouldn't let me do *anything* without permission. I felt constantly watched. I still feel that way when I'm with her."

A caller says, "I don't know whether my parents loved me or not. They had no way to express affection. I don't remember anyone ever hugging anyone else in my family."

Nancy, a colleague who was in therapy, said to me, "My father has always been depressed. Our whole relationship has consisted of my trying to get him out of his depression. That seems to be how we communicate: I'm still looking for a way to cure him."

I fell in love with Marianne. Not with the thirty-seven-year-old woman who was bitter and enraged at her mother—but with the six-year-old child underneath the rage and bitterness, the child who hoped that someone would fix her a snack when she came home from school.

"I lost my childhood," the woman raged.

But I don't think she did. She lost a *piece* of her childhood.

We all lose pieces. The child with an overprotective parent loses the piece that wants to take risks, to explore, to climb high fences, to perform daredevil stunts. If a child is never nurtured, that child loses the piece that can cuddle and be cuddled in return. The child who has always felt responsible for a depressed or addicted parent loses the piece of childhood that is carefree, out-of-control, irresponsible.

Whenever patients say, "My parents weren't loving enough," "My parents weren't respectful enough," "My parents weren't trusting enough," what they are addressing is the longing, underneath, that their parents *would* be "enough." Not to have a perfect parent is sad on two levels. It's sad because we live our childhood with a longing. And it's sad because we pay a price for that longing—relationships fail, addictions begin, depression recurs because we can't have what we long for.

And now: What do we do when we long for a piece of childhood that we never had? How do we make peace with the parents we have?

There's an old Sufi saying that I repeat often: "When the heart weeps for what it has lost, the soul rejoices for what it has discovered."

We weep for the pieces of childhood that we've lost—and weep for the price that we've paid. And as the weeping diminishes, we're able to discover not just what we lost but what we still own. I don't think we can make peace with our parents until after we've faced our pain, grieved the loss of the piece of childhood, and grieved the loss of the ideal parent. It is only then that we'll be able to find something in our parents that we can rejoice over—and perhaps begin, there, to celebrate the relationship that we have with them in the present.

When I was talking with Nancy, the colleague who had spent many years trying to "cure" her depressed father, I suggested that there might be some way she could feel closer to him without trying to relieve his depression. She agreed, but the way to do that eluded her. Her father had always been a difficult man to feel intimate with, and his advancing age did not change that. But as so often happens, a kind of answer emerged even as we were talking. We were discussing things that Nancy and her father might do together when I suggested, "Why don't you dance with him?"

As soon as I said those words, I started to cry. At first I didn't know why—but I thought I owed us both an explanation, and after a moment's reflection I said to Nancy, "I guess I chose dancing because that's probably the one thing I have missed most since my accident. And I'm painfully aware that I will never dance with either of my daughters at their weddings. It's almost as if I'm asking you to do something for me."

Her comment to me was that she had never felt more intimate with a man than she did at that moment. And she was able to take that experience of intimacy to her next visit with her father. She was able to talk to him about himself—about his wishes, his dreams, and his pain.

They danced. And while they danced, her long struggle to cure his depression was lifted. She could just enjoy being with him, in the immediate present, without trying to fix anything that had happened in the past.

PART TWO

❧

Our Mates

11

Falling in Love—the Great Hallucination

∾

In *The Good Apprentice*, the novelist and philosopher iris Murdoch wrote vividly about the pure experience of falling in love. The character who has this experience recalls it in terms of sensations that overwhelmed her at the moment when she was in the grip of its frenzy:

> Gradually she had felt her whole body change, first dreadfully chilled, then slowly warmed, by the rays which came from [him]. She had sat stiff at first with mingled horrified fear, misery, anger, embarrassment, remorse. . . . Then after a while she began to feel simply tired, surrendered to a hopeless quiet sense of "it's too much." Then a physical warmth began to steal over her and somehow, without altering her posture, she relaxed and let herself be warmed. She was conscious of an aura of emotion, unfocused desire, new desire. How could that be? There was a physical effect, a happening, as if her whole body were being remade, as if by radiation, the atoms of it changed. She felt soothed, as if ready for sleep, yet was also intensely alert, alive. . . . It was as if this were something beyond personality, a cosmic chemical change

wherein he was pure force and she was pure substance. So strong was her sense of impersonality, the ineluctable objectivity of the happening, that it could not have occurred to her then to wonder if [he] too were in any way conscious of it.

So goes love—that "cosmic chemical change" whereby human beings are reduced (or exalted) to "pure force" and "pure substance." And, above all, the "sense of impersonality."

This is the stuff of novels, poetry, song, drama—the "ineluctable objectivity of the happening"—the hallucination that depersonalizes, changing a flesh-and-blood, warts-and-all human being into a force that attracts so strongly that we are physically, emotionally, even spiritually changed by the experience.

We can even *see* the change in a person who has fallen in love. Shortly before I came across this passage, I had been treating a twenty-six-year-old woman who was dating a number of men. I recalled the day she came into my office with a silly grin on her face. Her eyes were glazed over. I thought, either she's started using drugs or . . .

"Carol, you're in love!" I guessed.

"Yeah—you're right," she responded with an even sillier grin. "How did you know?"

In love with *whom?*

Did she *know?* Did it *matter?*

I suspect that like so many people who fall in love, Carol was in love with falling-in-love. "He" (whoever he was) was pure force. "She" (with glazed eyes, joyous smile) was pure substance. Or vice versa. It didn't matter. Something ineluctable was *happening.* She was enchanted with whatever overwhelming process had just seized her, and—for whatever reason, by whatever means—her existence was illumined by it.

People who fall in love have a tendency to want to marry each other.

This is so self-evident that we don't question the logical connection between love and marriage. But marrying the person we've fallen in love with is actually a somewhat batty thing to do. "Falling in love" is, by its very nature, a transitory and temporary process—whereas everything about the marriage vow implies commitment and permanence. What this means is that any two people who fall in love and then get married are likely to be headed for some very confusing times.

Two psychologists joined me on *Voices in the Family* to talk about stages of relationships—Polly Young-Eisendrath, a Jungian analyst who does marriage counseling, and Ed Epstein, a clinical social worker who sees many couples in private practice.

"What *attracts* people to each other in the first place?" I asked. "What *makes* a couple? They say that marriages are made in the unconscious—not in heaven. But maybe they're both the same."

"The romance scheme that we have going now," said Polly, "is that you should go out and look for the person who throws you into a trance. After that, you hope for the best. You just *hope* that when you come out of the trance, this is somebody you like."

Of course, part of what we hope is that we'll never come out of the trance. We want the infatuation to continue forever and ever. As the trancelike, romantic stage of the relationship comes to an end, we may look for a new infatuation or try to hold on to the all-consuming passions of the fading romance.

But what if we marry the person we fell in love with? What if we have taken vows "for life" while we were under the illusion that the romance stage would last forever?

When we discussed stages of relationships, Ed Epstein observed that most marriages have a "predictable" first stage. "When two people get married, they are still having a romance. That lasts from a couple of months to maybe a year. But when the romance dies, what replaces it is a power-struggle stage. Sometimes, couples settle into a power struggle for the rest of their lives."

In the early days of marriage—when people are still in a trance, when love has transformed them into "pure force" and "pure substance"—the "impersonality" of love itself is so strong that neither can see the other clearly.

What can any therapist say to a twenty-six-year-old woman who has just fallen into this trancelike state?

The therapist is in a dilemma here. I would gladly introduce the impassioned people to each other—"introduce them," that is, in such a way that they could get to know each other on other levels before they start making lifelong commitments. As Polly commented—facetiously, yet wistfully—"Sometimes it seems to me that 'arranged' marriages might be easier." (But surely that's a therapist's wistfulness, arising from the fact that so many couples come to see us when they are in the later, troubled stages of getting-to-know-each-other.)

But no one is in a position to arbitrate love, and that's probably fortunate. People with the greatest illusions about each other can, in fact, become compatible lifelong companions. In the early stages of "falling in love," while the lovers are still "walking on air," who knows whether a match made in heaven and/or the unconscious will actually work? The best we can do is cross our fingers and hope that when the two people stop falling or floating, they find ways to begin a dialogue. As they get to know each other as human beings, perhaps they can become friends as well as lovers.

What about two people who were lucky enough to be close friends before they fell in love?

When we have a friend, be it male or female, the dynamics are much different from those in a love relationship. We accept that our friends have their own lives entirely apart from us. We may share confidences with them; we may become very close; but the friend is still just a friend. Nothing about *them* becomes part of us. Nothing is taken into the ego.

If we fall in love with that friend, we find other parts of our *selves* in the other person. Perhaps we find parts that are tender, passionate, nurturing, loving, or parts that are strong, forceful, courageous, daring. As we fall in love, those parts are absorbed into our core, our psyche. We love the feeling of completeness that we get when we are with the other person—as if there's no one else we need in all the world. Some parts of the other person that we just liked a lot when we were friends become essential to our very being when we fall in love.

And we begin to hallucinate. Distortions creep in. When John was just a friend of Jane's, perhaps she saw him as an energetic guy she liked to share things with. Now, what happens when she falls in love with him? She wants his dynamic energy to belong to her, to be hers exclusively, not shared with other people in the same way. John is part of her ego now; he helps to make her feel whole, complete, and wonderful. She can't help being jealous and possessive. He's carrying a part of her that she feels she needs for herself, at her very core. That's how the distortions are created.

Now that she's in love and she has taken part of him inside her, can she let go again? Can the friends-turned-lovers become just-friends again? What happens when the hallucination ends?

Ideally, Jane will work through the hallucination. She'll be able to accept John as someone whose energy goes up and down; whose temper is not always good-natured; whose character is far from perfect. And if John had the illusion that Jane would always care for him and nurture him, perhaps he'll discover the caring, nurturing parts of himself, so he won't need all of that from her. As the hallucinations diminish on both sides, perhaps they'll begin to see each other as they once were, as friends. And ideally they'll feel closer because of the wonderful feelings of "romance" they've experienced with each other, the hallucination they've shared together.

Whether or not friendship existed before the romance, what can be said with certainty is that the "falling in love" phase will always come to an end—rapidly or swiftly, by degrees or in one fell swoop. When the hallucinations are over, we will again be faced with the reality of our selves. And if we have made a commitment to the beloved, we will be faced with the reality of who *that* person is and what he or she wants.

What if our love relationships are repeatedly stuck in the "falling-in-love" stage? What if falling in love *with* love becomes an end in itself—and we become addicted to the glaze-eyed, silly-grinned high that we get when that happens?

When we do fall in love, I believe we are reaching for wholeness—the kind of wholeness that we had only when we were infants. It's been said that "we come alone into the world and leave it alone," but I don't think that's true: I think we come into the world very protected and cared for. The moment that nipple comes out of the mouth, we start yowling. And we spend the rest of our lives waiting to feel as connected as we were back then.

Yes—even the classic "playboy," the freewheeling "ladies' man," needs to feel connected.

I suppose my patient would have to be classified as a Don Juan. Ray was strikingly good-looking, in the craggy mode of a TV actor—Tom Selleck comes to mind. Women found him fascinating.

When Ray first started seeing me, he had just ended his relationship with Clarissa, to whom he had been married for about a year. His description of the affairs he'd had since then reminded me of a shark in a feeding frenzy. He'd had numerous one-night stands and "fallen in love" with every woman he'd slept with.

Ray loved the sensation of being in love. But when he felt himself being swallowed up in a relationship—giving too much of himself—he backed off. He was disappointed that his marriage to Clarissa had failed. But when he looked back at "what went wrong," he concluded that she had been "too demanding," that she "wanted too much" from him.

In therapy, Ray did a lot of work with his family of origin. Ray was the middle of three brothers. The older one was the prince, the overachiever. He always did well in school and sports. By the time he was in high school, he was so popular, active, and studious that he spent little time at home. And after he left for college, the family rarely heard from him. Ray's younger brother was schizophrenic. During the years Ray was growing up, that brother had required constant treatment and occasional hospitalization.

His parents had a horrible marriage. They didn't even like each other. Ray said that his father was so withdrawn, he wouldn't even have dinner with the rest of the family.

Ray didn't know how to have a relationship because he never saw one. He was terribly lonely in the family. With his father totally withdrawn, his older brother busy being "the prince," and his younger brother ill, Ray was left to take care of his mother.

Emotionally, Ray's mother had no husband and no other children but Ray. She was angry at Ray and everyone else. He felt overpowered and guilty in that relationship, and he felt responsible for ameliorating her anger, which of course he couldn't do. So Ray's relationship with his mother became his burden. He was both afraid of her and angry at her at the same time.

Because of Ray's good looks, women were always after him—and he rushed into these relationships as a way to cure the loneliness. But he never felt safe in these relationships because he had never felt safe in the family. He was always afraid he might be overwhelmed by the women he dated, burdened by their need and anger. And he was half-stuck in his relationship with his mother. Part of him was still with her, carrying her burden and believing he could save her.

During therapy, his mother came in for several sessions. She talked to Ray and to me about her life. Ray saw that she was angry and depressed and that she would probably remain so for the rest of her life. He recognized his powerlessness in that relationship, and he realized the hopelessness of trying to make his mother's life better for her. Just knowing that—having a better understanding of his own powerlessness—helped Ray to free the part that had become stuck trying to save his mother.

Would his "feeding frenzy" pattern of dating ever change? Would he ever be satisfied in a relationship with a woman?

When I asked him what would happen if he were not able to date—if women didn't find him attractive—he thought for a while and said, "I'd be terribly lonely."

I said to him, "Aren't you anyway?"

He looked down for a moment and said, "Yes, I've always been."

I told him, "Well, I'm lonely, too."

"You are?" He was astounded.

"Yes, of course. Isn't everybody?"

"Being in love" helped Ray not to feel his very painful loneliness. Every time he fell in love, he felt whole. When he could make peace with that part of his loneliness instead of running away from it, he stopped being afraid of being swallowed up by another person. (The truth of the matter is that he was really afraid that he was so hungry and so desperate that he would swallow up the other person. But, of course, it was easier to blame her!)

In talking about his family of origin, Ray had begun to find a self that he had not recognized before. He had discovered that he would never "fix" the family, heal his mother, or rescue anyone from his unhappiness. And when he realized that he was powerless to change any of them, he felt safer about himself. Perhaps that "self" would not disappear, after all, if he were committed to a relationship.

He and Clarissa were later remarried.

What I'm getting at is the distinction between *falling* in love and *being* in love.

When we fall in love, we may be "walking on air." We may feel "ten feet tall." Our "hearts beat faster." We "live and die" for the other person, give that person "everything," are overwhelmed by the feeling that we can "become one" with that person. Every cliché *about* falling in love is likely to ring true when you *are* falling in love.

Being in love is different. It means loving another human being, not just loving a feeling. It means rejoicing in the other person's life; it means being connected and staying connected. When we stay in love, the hallucination fades, but we become in touch with the real person. We discover how to find that person lovable, and we risk ourselves in the loving.

Carol, the twenty-six-year-old patient who fell in love, eventually got to the stage of *being* in love—but only after she went through a whole variety of stages beforehand.

First she became very frightened by the relationship. Falling in love made her feel dependent and vulnerable. "Will he hurt me?" she wondered. Out of that anxiety came other questions, as she started to wonder about herself: "Will I hurt him? Will I leave him? What about my own destructive impulses?"

Carol and her boyfriend, Evan, moved in together. Now she discovered for certain that she had *not* met the perfect man! As they began sharing apartment life, he became a warts-and-all human being, and some of the warts Carol didn't like. It turned out Evan was compulsive about what time he went to bed, so he didn't like to go out and party. Carol found out that he liked to have his socks folded a certain way. For a while, these things enraged her. She was very angry at him for not being perfect.

I invited Carol to bring Evan into therapy. As they talked about themselves and each other, Evan became more of a person to her. Did Carol like this person or not?

Gradually she fell in love with him again. She began to value who he was. She realized he wasn't the perfect man, but that didn't frighten her so much. She thought his quirks were cute.

In past relationships, she had always run away when the man "let her down," when his quirks had begun to annoy her and his imperfections had made her angry. This time, she went through all those stages of falling in love and came to a stage that had eluded her before—the stage of *being* in love.

12

Our Fantasy of the Marriage

∾

Considering what's at stake, the marriage ceremony is breathtakingly short. After all the preparation—the anxiety, the expectations—suddenly we're ready for the moment. The vows are spoken, the kiss exchanged, and the couple, holding hands, ventures forth on their great journey of life together.

But if one could peer for a moment into the conscious and unconscious thoughts of the participants during those exhilarating moments of vow taking, I wonder what we'd actually hear. Perhaps something like this:

"I, TOM . . . (I wonder if she really knows what I'm like) . . . TAKE YOU, SUSAN . . . (She's perfect—everything I want in a wife) . . . TO BE MY WEDDED WIFE . . . (I know Mom and Dad are happy with her) . . . TO HAVE AND TO HOLD . . . (Am I really the man I'm supposed to be? Can I really do this?) . . . IN SICKNESS AND IN HEALTH . . . (She really understands me— she's going to take care of me) . . . TILL DEATH DO US PART."

"I, SUSAN . . . (I can really be myself with Tom) . . . TAKE YOU, TOM . . . (He gets along so well with everyone) . . . TO BE MY WEDDED HUSBAND . . . (We're going to have such a happy family) . . . TO HAVE AND TO HOLD . . . (He's honest and serious) . . . IN SICKNESS AND IN HEALTH . . . (I feel so secure) . . . TILL DEATH DO US PART."

Clifford Sager, author of The Marriage Contract, suggests that we make three kinds of contracts when we pick our mates.

The first is the conscious, verbalized contract that we hear at weddings: "I'll take care of you and you take care of me."

The second is the conscious, nonverbalized contract, which includes the thoughts and feelings that we're really too ashamed to talk about. The nonverbalized part of the contract might be "I need you to always be self-confident and positive, so I can feel good about myself." Or it might be a request for protection and security, such as "I'm really scared of adulthood. Will you take care of me?" Or it could be a "contract" for constant love: "I'm scared that I won't be able to take care of you when you need me to. Will you love me anyway?" Or "Will you love me when you know about my fears and my vulnerabilities?"

The third kind of contract is unconscious, involving all the expectations that each person brings to the relationship. This unconscious material is, by definition, negative. Unlike the conscious parts of the marriage contract, the unconscious material is just too frightening for us to be aware of. It doesn't sound pretty. A woman's *unconscious* expectation might arise from past experiences in her own family of origin: "I expect you to be the bastard my father was," or "I expect you to go out and drink and screw women and victimize me—so I'll have to be a martyr." And buried in the man's unconscious might be the expectation "You'll be demanding and possessive, like all the other women I've known."

With so many contracts at the beginning of a marriage, what are we really wishing for and expecting—and what is our mate really wishing for us? Often, we don't even know.

Tom and Susan agreed to come into the studio for an interview and therapy session that would be recorded and later aired on the radio show. Their relationship had reached an important point. After eight years of marriage, their first daughter, Rachel, had recently been born. At the time of the interview, she was just three months old.

Tom, thirty-three, was a hospital administrator. Susan, two years younger, had been a paralegal, but she had stopped working during pregnancy and was now a full-time mother. Both had grown up in Philadelphia, and their families of origin still lived in the area.

Susan had been introduced to Tom by one of his sisters, a friend of hers. "It wasn't love at first sight," said Susan. They had three years of what she called "courtship" before they were married. While they were going together, Tom left for Mexico to work in the Peace Corps. Though Susan visited him as often as she could, she said she was miserable during that time. She missed Tom, and she was lonely. When they were married, Tom was twenty-five and had three more years to serve in the Peace Corps. Susan moved to Mexico with him.

In a way, many of their expectations about the marriage were put on hold while they were in Mexico—a fact neither of them fully recognized until they came back to Philadelphia. As long as they were living in a foreign country, on temporary assignment, far away from their families, as Tom said, "Some issues got put on the back burner." Before they could begin to resolve those issues or even face them, Tom and Susan had to find out what their fantasies of each other and of the marriage were. But first of all, they had to recognize that they *had* fantasies.

Susan came from a close-knit family whom she loved to be with. All her images of family gatherings were positive. She had always imagined marrying someone who would feel perfectly at home in her family's midst; he would be a willing, gentle father, and they would raise wonderful, happy children.

She also knew what kind of marriage she wanted to avoid. "I had two older sisters who were in difficult marriages. They were having hard times with the men they were married to. I knew those men didn't enjoy being with my family. And I really felt I wanted to find someone who would love to be with my family and help me feel comfortable. Tom fit in well."

Tom was a man whom everyone seemed to approve of. (After all, his own sister had praised him to Susan—that's what initially stirred her interest in him.) Honest, smart, sensitive—he was the exact image of what Susan thought a perfect husband should be.

And what did he expect of her? I asked Tom what had been his fantasy of the woman he had married. "I thought Susan would support the things I wanted to do in my life. My fantasy was that she would be independent in her own way—though we would have an interdependence in our marriage. We wouldn't impinge too much on each other, but each would be supportive of what the other was doing."

I asked them both how it worked out.

"I was terribly unhappy," said Susan. "I felt betrayed by this person because he wasn't living up to my expectations of him." As she said that, there was a sad smile on her face.

"Feelings of betrayal are real important," I said. "Even though he didn't betray anything that he promised, or that you verbalized, he did betray your hopes, your dreams—he betrayed the myth."

Susan agreed. "I grew up with a fairy-tale story called 'What It's Like to Be Married,'" she said. "That story always had a cheerful, smiling mom; a perfect daddy; and lots of happy children running around. *That* was the story in my head—and I had to see that it was a complete myth."

Five years into the marriage, Tom said, he felt he was "married to two different people. Sometimes we really enjoyed ourselves and our families. We would have a really good time. Then issues came up—the issues of family, of boundaries . . . "

Tom was unhappy spending so much time with Susan's family, and he fought by withdrawing into silence. Susan fought by "getting bossy" and "saying mean things." As so many of us do, Susan and Tom had each learned to fight in the families they grew up with; they had learned by watching their parents.

Susan said that Tom was reluctant to talk, and because of that, she said, "Our fights were just misery."

I asked what their fights would have sounded like if both could have taken "a magic cure pill."

"I would have said that I was absolutely livid, furious," said Tom. "I would have told her I needed more space for my own needs."

And Susan?

"I would have told him I was feeling betrayed by this person because he just hadn't lived up to my expectations."

Then why had each one picked the other as a mate?

Each of them, in some way, needed the other to feel "complete" or "whole."

"Susan was vivacious and outgoing," said Tom. "She made up for some of my reclusive characteristics. In some ways I thought of her as a gift that I was bringing to my own family. She helped me feel better with them."

And Tom had a role to play in making Susan feel whole. "Tom constantly puts me to the test to be honest," said Susan. "I have a tendency to just stay on 'the fun side' and not really delve into things. He draws out the serious side of me—which I appreciate."

So Tom had unfinished business in his family; he needed the outgoing, vivacious "personality" who would be a "gift" to his family—and make him feel more significant to them. And Susan wanted Tom's seriousness to round herself out.

Each of them was trying to marry different parts of themselves. Inevitably, that leads to difficulty. We can't find a missing part *outside* ourselves; we have to find it within. Whenever we *apparently* find it on the outside, there are always flaws or problems with it. In addition, when we marry a mate who seems to provide or "make up" the part we're missing, that's all we can see of our mate—that one part. We don't see that person as he or she really is.

As Susan and Tom began their eighth year of marriage, now with a child in the equation, they were still coming to terms with the fact that neither of them was going to live up to the fantasy of an ideal partner. Each was changing, of course—and both becoming better acquainted with the person they had married. They had begun to recognize their fantasies, take responsibility for them, and not expect the other to change to fit the role of the mythical husband or mythical wife.

Were they happier for coming to this recognition and taking responsibility for their fantasies? Yes and no. It wasn't happiness in the conventional sense of "happily ever after." After all, there was grief, too—and loss. Tom had to give up the dream of bringing home to his family the perfect, vivacious wife who would take care of everything for him. And Susan had to forfeit the illusion that, among other things, Tom would make her feel like a more "serious person."

What they found in therapy was some validation of the truths that they had perhaps known about each other all along. It was as if someone had said to them, "You're right—you are two people who will never make a perfect fit. Whatever you feel lacking will never be filled in by the other person." To recognize that about each other was a struggle. It was painful. They both felt loss, and then relief. And the discovery was sometimes joyous.

That's what happens when we lose some things and find new ones. We painfully give up the hallucination; we ruin the nice gossamer that we wrapped around our partner and around the relationship. What we find instead is something more solid and more anchored—and that's where we discover the joyousness.

I think anyone who gets married is certain to have private fantasies about his marriage. Yet few of us are *aware* of those fantasies—we don't really know why we chose the mate we did. At the beginning of marriage, we have wishes, dreams, hopes, expectations, and assumptions that are too numerous to name. Usually, if we come from a family that we like, our fantasy is that we are going to re-create that family by making an "ideal" marriage. And if we come from a family that has difficulties, our fantasy is that our new family will be an improvement.

In either case, we "expect" something impossible of our mate—that this person will help us improve on our family of origin or will collaborate in creating a perfectly mirrored reproduction of it. But initially, the last thing we expect of our mates is that they will end up being exactly like themselves.

Ideally, that final expectation will come with time.

13

Secrets Kept, Secrets Shared

∾

When I interviewed Tom and Susan for *Voices in The Family,* I asked them about the secrets that each had carried into their marriage.

Susan recalled, "I couldn't bear the idea that I wouldn't have kids. I thought I would have to get out of the marriage if Tom wouldn't have children with me. One criterion of a 'good husband' was that he would also be a 'wonderful father.'"

Tom, on the other hand, had been *terrified* of having children. Four years into the marriage, when he began talking to a therapist, he discovered why he was so afraid: "I realized my own childhood had been filled with feelings of abandonment and rage. My sense of being a child was a sense of being in terror. I didn't want to inflict those feelings on a child of my own."

As I talked with Tom and Susan during the taping session, I could watch their three-month-old daughter, Rachel, playing happily in the room adjacent to the studio. So Susan had "won"—they now had a child.

The surprise was that Tom had also won. "I have a tremendous sense of relief," he told me. "I discovered that my child doesn't have to feel afraid and abandoned. And I found out I could go back in my own mind and comfort myself. Now I feel like I have two children. One is me—I can 'hold myself' and give myself all the attention I didn't get as a child. The other is Rachel. When I rock her to sleep at night, I'm rocking both of my 'children' to sleep."

Susan and Tom each had parts of themselves that made them feel uncomfortable, ashamed, or fearful. Susan was afraid that she would never feel complete—never feel like "a whole woman"— unless she had children. That secret frightened her. What if her husband never wanted to have children? What if her only choice was to leave him or to give up her own hope of ever feeling like a "whole person"? (Of course, we know the truth—that a woman can feel like a whole person without having children. But this was not the way Susan felt.) As long as Susan stayed in this marriage, only Tom could give her children; only Tom could make her feel like the whole person she wanted to be.

And Tom had a secret that he was ashamed of. He felt his childhood was not history; he feared that he would re-create his own feelings of abandonment if he were to become a father. At a deeper level, Tom felt Susan or a baby should redo his own childhood.

Beyond the feelings that they shared with each other were other feelings kept to themselves. Ideally, perhaps, they would share everything—they would be completely known to each other. In reality, as much as they needed to be known to each other at the deepest level, they never would or could be.

Part of what we do when we're married is look to our mate to make ourselves whole. Susan expected Tom to make her a "whole woman." Tom expected Susan to redo his childhood. But, of course, these were the fantasies they had about each other.

And each of them had fantasies about themselves. In Susan's fantasy, she was the loving, tender, capacious mother happily ensconced in an Ozzie-and-Harriet family. Tom had a fantasy of himself as a successful, independent world traveler who had the freedom to undertake exotic journeys and have great adventures.

Once they gave up their fantasies of each other, then they were left with what was incomplete in themselves. Like their fantasies about each other, the fantasies about themselves would never be realized. Could they live with that incompleteness? Could they share the feelings of incompleteness with each other? If so, then each of them would be more whole.

Think how much more powerful each of us will be if we can be aware of what's incomplete inside ourselves.

One of the reasons that secrets stay secret is that they're parts of ourselves that we're uncomfortable with, we're ashamed of, or we're afraid of.

In the beginning of the relationship, we fall in love with the fantasy of the "ideal" man or the "ideal" woman. The relationship runs into trouble when we believe *we* are our mate's ideal. We might think, "My mate *sees me* as a strong and competent person. If he knows that I often feel empty and inadequate, then he won't love me anymore." The problem with that thinking is that we actually believe we have to be perfect in order to keep our mate happy. And that means keeping secrets.

When we share our secrets—share the vulnerable parts of ourselves—we're letting the other person see our flaws and imperfections. In the early stages of a relationship, we might not wish to show our partner the vulnerable parts of ourselves. We might not wish to acknowledge that we have those secret parts. But as a relationship matures, we're really withholding parts of ourselves, both from our mate and from ourselves, if we are striving to be "perfect." We are in a relationship in which we're not whole.

Sandy and I were married when I was twenty-three years old and she was twenty. She always looked up to me, which made me feel strong, smart, and competent. From me she got a feeling of safety and of being protected because she saw me as the "good father." From her I got feelings of manliness and strength because she was the "good daughter" who saw me as the ideal man.

Four years after we were married, Sandy was diagnosed with malignant melanoma. Since neither of us knew whether she would recover, we had to say good-bye to each other before she went into the hospital. And at the same time, we had to say good-bye to our fantasies about each other. I could no longer make believe that I was the big strong man and she was the little girl. We were forced to face our lives and our deaths. The secrets couldn't be kept anymore. I had to talk about my fear, sadness, and vulnerability, and she did, too. At that point, all we could be to each other was two human beings stripped of our artificial roles.

Sandy recovered, and for a number of years we got back into the old system of my being the stronger one and her being the weaker one. Then I broke my neck. And there were times when she literally held me in her arms as I wept and wondered about my life. Those were times when I felt more intimate with her than I have felt with any other human being.

At such a moment, when we're at our most vulnerable, our most intimate, there are no more secrets. There can't be.

Once we reveal the parts of ourselves that we're ashamed of and we're embarrassed about, we have a better sense of ourselves and a better sense of what we want to keep private and what we want to share. But as long as we have too many parts of ourselves that seem shameful and embarrassing, we're going to get them all confused with what is private.

Once I shared all my vulnerability with Sandy, once I gave up my secrets, I ultimately came to make peace with the idea that the way I experienced my life was something that nobody could understand. People can guess about the way I experience my pain, my frustration, my anguish. But ultimately, those are my secrets. Ideally, I would like people to connect with my experience, my soul. But I know it will never happen. Once I'm able to give up trying to get that unattainable connection, I can better enjoy the relationships and intimacy that I do have.

14

Sexual Issues: Living with Change

ॐ

In many marriages, sex becomes a metaphor for what's going on in the relationship and within each partner. Sometimes, sex is a battleground. At other times, it may represent power and control, punishment, or a test of wills. And it's even a test of love.

Ideally, as a marriage matures, our sexuality also matures. As we become more aware of our own needs and more comfortable with what pleases us, we also get to know our mates better and we become more comfortable understanding what pleases them sexually. And as we fall in love with the human being, our love becomes more spiritual. Loving the person becomes more important than our love for their body, their orgasm, or our own orgasm.

But that's the ideal. What happens when sex doesn't feel as wonderful as it did when we were madly in love? What if once-erotic experiences no longer arouse us? What if wrinkles start to bother us—or even worse, what if *our own* wrinkles start to bother us—so our sexual partners seem less appealing than they were? Often, the sense of loss is profound, because our own sexuality is an important part of our emotional lives. Sometimes it's confusing; sometimes it's frightening; sometimes it's infuriating.

And we do whatever we can to recapture what was a wonderful experience.

I think sex is a loaded issue because we're naked in so many ways. In the act of sex, we're at our most vulnerable. And if sex doesn't feel wonderful or just isn't happening anymore, how do we sort out all the issues we have with our mate and with our marriage?

Karen Brash, a registered nurse and certified sex counselor, was a guest on my show, sharing her views on how men and women express their sexuality. Noting that well over half of all happily married couples say that they are "disappointed" in their sex lives, Karen said, "There's a tendency in this supersexed culture to think that everyone else is sexually satisfied and stimulated . . . except *me*."

Karen had worked extensively in a medical center with people who had health problems or were disabled.

"I've begun to think about what it is that helps us to be healthy. And to me it's several things.

"First is knowing yourself—what you need and what you want. Sometimes *being held* is all you really want, and sometimes you may want something different from that.

"The other part is being able to *communicate* what you want. Most people, I find, still don't have a language to communicate their sexual needs. As a culture, we're still sexually illiterate. I wish we could cultivate a language to talk about sex—so we wouldn't worry about finding the right words. I wish we had a language of feeling, so that we could express what we want with our partners.

"And the other thing that we need to remember about sexual health is that we don't have to be stuck in rigid stereotypes of what it means to be masculine or feminine. I would hope that we can express the masculine *and* feminine in each of us—both parts, as we wish, whenever we wish, whether we're male or female."

Barry and Kate had been married fifteen years when Barry was diagnosed as having multiple sclerosis. Partly as a result of his illness, he was having difficulty with his erections. Barry was depressed—he felt like less of a man in the marriage—and Kate's reassurances just felt maternal. The words that she hoped would be reassuring only contributed to his feelings of impotence. Every time Kate asked to make love, Barry felt performance anxiety. In the past, Barry had often been the one to initiate sex. Now, he never asked, and eventually Kate began to question whether she was sexually appealing.

After they had talked about their recent unsuccessful attempts at sexual intimacy, we discussed doing some things differently.

"When you go to bed," I suggested, "why don't you try getting undressed and looking at each other. Touch each other and talk about how the touch feels to you. Can you explore what makes you feel good and what makes you feel bad?"

I told Barry and Kate that for about the first year after my accident, I had grieved for my physical and sexual losses. It seemed that every time Sandy and I attempted to make love, I couldn't do it because I didn't feel like a man. When my wife took my clothes off, I felt like her child. How could she respect me if she had to take my clothes off, as she would a baby's! How could I please her?

During that stage of grief, I realized that what I had to do was think more about me than about her. Trying to guess about her losses was almost self-serving, because it meant I could avoid my own. I had to grieve my loss of ability to undress her, to be on top, to perform as I always thought a man was supposed to perform. I had to grieve my loss of sensation. All of these things had died and needed to be mourned.

But as I closed the doors on sexuality (as I had once defined it), new doors opened. Once I had grieved and focused on my own losses, I felt more centered and more able to hear about Sandy's losses without the fear that they would destroy me. Furthermore, when I was ready to hear about her losses, she was finally able to talk about them without being protective of me and fearful of how "fragile" I was.

Something else happened. When I was able to nurture Sandy as she talked about her losses, I felt like more of a man than I ever had before. I had lost all the artificial "ornaments" of manhood, such as the ability to be on top and the ability to be able to undress my wife. But I was left with the ability to nurture my wife through her losses, and because of that, I felt exquisitely masculine.

The first time after my accident that Sandy and I made love, she moved her hands below my shoulders, where I had lost sensation, and I immediately said, "Don't touch me where I'm dead." It was only after I had grieved that death that I was able to see what life there was beneath my shoulders. Only then were she and I both able to use my whole body.

Could Barry and Kate explore what felt good and what felt bad? Could they find out where and how they wanted to touch each other and be touched?

If you're a man, can you explore what it means to be a sexual man? Does it mean conquest and orgasm? Are they part of a real definition? What is a man, anyway? And if you're a woman, can you be a sexual woman if you're not being seduced? Can you appreciate your own sexuality just because it's there? What are your definitions of sexuality? Does sex mean power or control to you?

Barry and Kate began to explore in some of the ways we had discussed. For the first six months Barry did not want Kate to be near his penis. He had to teach her how he felt—and eventually it was okay. And Kate had to educate Barry about the importance of intimacy and touch, which were more important to her than orgasm.

In therapy Kate was able to say to her husband, "I love you—and I love your body and I love your soul." And she asked him angrily, "Do you think your penis is really that important to me?" Now Barry was able to hear her, believe her, and trust her. He was also able to say, "My penis *is* important to *me*." So Kate could appreciate how great his loss was. And he, finally, could appreciate that loss of touch and intimacy was much sadder to her than his difficulty with having an erection.

A few years after therapy, Kate wrote me a letter to ask how I was. In the letter she said things were still going well for Barry and her.

"When we go to bed," she wrote, "we're still talking, and things are still changing."

And I thought: That's what mature sex is all about.

Ideally, things will never stop changing.

I think change begins when we start talking.

But in order to begin talking about sex, it's important to understand why you *haven't* for all these years.

Is it because you feel anxious or frightened? Because you don't know what your own needs are? Are you afraid of your mate's response? We need to find a vocabulary. We can't rely on "guessing" what our partner wants, nor expect a partner to interpret mute signs and signals.

If you are a man, perhaps sex means that you have been accepted at the most intimate level by a woman. And if your wife doesn't want to make love, doesn't that make you feel unloved and rejected? For many men, sex is a vehicle, a way to achieve intimacy. And a woman's refusal to have sex is felt as a refusal to *be* intimate.

But sex can mean the complete opposite to a woman—and often does. If you are a woman who needs to feel intimate and safe and trusting before you can be happy with sex, then you need other kinds of closeness. You need the intimacy that comes through holding, talking, and touching.

Where do we find the vocabulary to meet each other and talk about our differences? I don't think you have to know any of the answers before you begin to talk about your sexual needs.

But it helps to say, "I need to talk about something and I'm frightened of your response." And you can add, "I feel terribly uncomfortable, ashamed, and embarrassed. But I need you just to listen and then I need you to talk to me about yourself."

And from that point on—you just fumble your way through, the way you did the first time you made love.

15

From Johnandmary to John and Mary

∾

My guest, Dr. Edward Monte, was a senior staff clinician at the Marriage Council of Philadelphia. During one of my shows, I asked him to describe some of the stages that people go through in a marriage:

"During the blissful period—when we're falling in love, first living together, getting engaged, or getting married—we give up chunks of our identity. We want to fit in with our mate and make something new. It's exciting and wonderful to find someone who fills in some of the gaps that we feel in ourselves. But this is where we lose track of where *I* begin and end, and where my *partner* begins and ends.

"Often the couple takes on a new name—Johnandmary. It all becomes one name. For a while, people don't hear much about John without hearing about Mary. Now there's a couple with a single identity. If those people are in their twenties, they are really just beginning to understand what it means to be an adult. So there is a conflict between 'Am I an individual?' and 'Am I part of this unit that everyone now identifies as a couple?'"

Many couples *want* to think of themselves in just that way— as Johnandmary, a single, inseparable unit. Isn't this the "ideal" of romantic love? We find the partner whom we wish to bond with for the rest of our lives—the person who makes us feel whole—and we strive to become "at one" with that person.

When we fall in love for the first time, we feel that the other person is part of our very soul and that all parts of us are integrated. But that feeling of "wholeness" doesn't seem to last. The intimacy of Johnandmary changes as each of them—John, Mary—recovers a separate identity again. Yet they are still linked to each other emotionally. And, in some ways, they are inevitably linked to each other's identity. How does a couple make it through this stage of changing identities? How do they resolve the conflicts between being one and being separate?

In *We: Understanding the Psychology of Romantic Love,* the noted Jungian analyst Robert A. Johnson analyzes the archetypal love story in Western literature, the story of Tristan and Isolte. As the relationship of these passionate lovers begins to mature, they reach a stage that is analogous to the "Johnandmary" stage. For Tristan and Isolte, there are many possibilities for development in their evolving relationship. In fact, the potential is greater than ever before. Can they achieve separation from each other—and, in the same evolution of their relationship, realize the potential for a new connectedness and relatedness that they never had before? Johnson describes the dilemma in this way:

An awesome potential is at stake in this evolution. It is the potential for being fully individual while also relating genuinely to a fellow human being. It is . . . by putting his own soul back inside himself that a man wakes up to the fact of his individuality. In becoming aware that there is a part of himself that can't be lived through another person, for which he must take responsibility on his own, he awakens to the unexpected extensity and complexity of his individual self. In turn, as he awakens to his own uniqueness, he becomes capable of relating directly to a woman in her individuality. *The test of true individuation is that it include the capacity to relate to another person and to respect him or her as an individual.* [Italics mine.]

Intimacy is something that we all crave, but it's something that we all fear to a greater or lesser degree. Why do we crave it? Because it makes us feel whole, connected, a part of something outside ourselves. It makes the world feel safe. And for some of us, the intimacy of becoming "one" with another person is our first experience with loving and feeling loved.

Why, then, with all these wonderful potentialities, does intimacy so often feel frightening? Well, I think there are many things about intimacy that *are* frightening. With greater intimacy, we become more open to *being known*. But being known raises fearful questions: Will you still love me if you know me? And *how much* am I willing to be known? There are also questions of *trust:* How much can I trust you? How much can I trust myself?

What did intimacy mean in the family you grew up with? If one or both of your parents were all over you, checking up on you, looking into your private business, then intimacy might mean loss of control. And that would be frightening. If you grew up in a family where you felt harmed, abused, or abandoned, intimacy could mean fear of harming someone else, fear of being harmed, or fear of abandonment. Those, too, are frightening qualities.

At first, it may feel very good to trust our mate blindly. But after a while, that kind of intimacy can make us feel out of control—and loss of control feels frightening. Then come the power struggles. We may want to control our mate, so we won't feel so frightened, but that need for control is really a need to feel in control of ourselves.

How do we reach a balance between the need to control and the need for intimacy—the need to become part of something else and at the same time to become our own person?

A young woman, recently married, was struggling with this question when she called in to *Voices in the Family*. For her, the issue was a financial matter—who should "control" the bank account. When she was first married, she had put her own money into a joint account with her husband's. That action represented all the trust she was placing in the marriage. By "giving up" her own bank account, she was showing her husband how much faith she had in him and in their relationship. But now she was having second thoughts.

I asked her to describe her husband.

"I guess you could say I married my opposite," she said. "My husband is strong in a lot of areas—he's a very good listener and communicator. I think he is someone who values my thoughts and feelings. He's very nonjudgmental, and this has helped me to grow a lot.

"But his financial ways are the opposite of mine. His attitude is *'Don't worry about it. We'll take care of it tomorrow,'* whereas I have always been very thrifty, saving, and careful. He is kind of a laid-back person—and I have always been very meek and proper."

"And if you could put both of you in a bottle and shake you up," I suggested, "it would be wonderful."

She laughed. "That's right. But the hardest thing for me is to let go and take a leap of faith. I tried. I closed down my own savings account and put my money into our joint account. It was very hard for me to say, 'Okay, we're going to make it. This is what I'm bringing to the marriage, and I'm going to have to trust my husband that he's not going to squander this money.'"

"Is he in charge?" I asked.

"Well, he writes the checks. But we've had a problem establishing *how* we should pay our bills. My philosophy is that we pay them all off when the bill comes in—you don't carry it over."

"What does money mean to you?" I asked.

"Security," she answered instantly. "It doesn't mean *things*."

She talked about a period during college when she had been hospitalized for a long illness. When she came out of the hospital, she said, she'd had to spend all her savings on doctors' bills. As a result, she had been forced to go back and live with her parents after she graduated.

Since security was so important to her, I asked why she had chosen to close down her savings account. "Because I didn't want to keep my money away from him," she answered. "I didn't want to say, 'No, you can't spend this.'"

So John's bank account and Mary's bank account had become Johnandmary's bank account. And what had become of Mary's separate need—the need for her own security?

"For whatever reason," I said, "you have your issues with money, and you have to respect those issues in yourself. And if keeping your savings account can allay your anxiety, I think you should do it.

"But there's a relationship issue in there that's more important than the money. When you say 'Money means security,' I think you're asking your husband a question. And that question is, 'Are you going to take care of me emotionally?' That's probably what he's wondering, too—and that's what needs to be addressed in the marriage."

In this life we cannot gain anything unless we're willing to give up something. That euphoric feeling that we have when we become a Johnandmary has to be given up if we want to reclaim ourselves, our identity, our autonomy. You have to be willing to give up that wonderful hallucinatory sense of intimacy. And if you reclaim yourself, you're just going to have to trust that a new relationship will ensue.

We all enter relationships with fantasies and expectations—and most of them are unrealistic. If we're able to give up some of our expectations and become two separate people, the relationship will no longer be the ideal, but it will certainly have room to grow. John will be happier with himself; Mary will be happier with herself; and therefore both will bring much more to this new relationship.

16

Power Struggles:
What Does *He* Want? What Does *She* Want?

ॐ

In many respects, men and women are exquisitely opposite. But often we don't realize how opposite until we try to live together. Perhaps men and women always want different things, or we want the same things, but in different ways. In any case, we often use different languages, so the problems of trying to get what we want are infinitely complicated by the difficulty of saying exactly what we need.

When there's a problem with the relationship and someone calls a therapist, ninety percent of the time it's the woman. To me that's a signal that the woman is in charge of "managing" the relationship. But the difference between men and women goes further than that. Once the couple is in my office, usually the woman wants to *talk about* the problem and the man wants to *fix* it. She says, "You're not listening to me!" And he says, "So what am I supposed to *do*?" And until they start to use the same language, it's unlikely that either one of them will know what the other is really saying.

But, today, there's also another factor in many of the conversations that take place between men and women—and that's the women's movement. I think many men are angry because they feel threatened by the movement and abandoned by their wives. Women, on the other hand, are trying very hard not to end up like their mothers—they're working hard at careers, motherhood, *and* relationships. But they're not necessarily having a good time, either. And many are feeling hurt.

Julie is a very articulate and pretty thirty-five-year-old nurse. She married Ben in 1975. Although Julie originally chose nursing because it was "acceptable" for women, she has always enjoyed her profession. Early in the marriage, she and Ben had two children. Julie continued to work, and even though she was very busy, she enjoyed both the kids and her career. Now that the children have reached adolescence, Julie has begun to look seriously at the marriage—perhaps for the first time.

Ben, a good-looking man with a close-cropped beard, is a forty-year-old lawyer. In general, his conversation is more reserved than Julie's. He chooses his words carefully. Occasionally, he glances at the clock to see how much time is left. I am immediately struck by the contrasting expressions on their faces. Ben comes into the session looking frightened and angry, eyes narrowed. Julie looks at me wide-eyed, in more obvious pain.

Julie is unhappy with Ben in many ways, and she has been trying to change him for years. Now she's considering divorce.

"Ben is *never* emotional," she says. "He just doesn't respond at all. It feels like I'm living with a man who's wearing a mask. I never know what's behind it."

"I don't know what the hell she's talking about," says Ben. "I've done everything she wants. What am I supposed to do—end my career and devote my life to her?"

It's been more than a year since they made love.

Julie's demands take the form of complaints. "He works all the time," she says. "He's never at home with the kids. . . . Whenever I try to talk about what's going on with me, he doesn't listen—all he wants to do is fix whatever is wrong. . . . He's totally preoccupied with himself and his work. . . . He doesn't respect my work and he doesn't respect my needs."

As Julie is talking, Ben shuts down. He folds his arms and looks at Julie without responding.

When I ask Ben what it's like to be in this marriage, he says Julie tries to manipulate and control him. He complains that she's not sexual. "She's totally preoccupied with herself and what she needs," he says, adding, "I don't think she pays enough attention to the kids, either."

Julie says this is the type of answer she expects from Ben. He's unavailable to her. The more she tries to talk to him, the less available he becomes. She sees no alternative but to end the marriage.

I ask Julie and Ben to talk about the families they grew up in. Julie says she was one of three children. "My mother used to tell me that she 'almost' went to college, but she married my dad instead," says Julie. "I think she always felt like she missed out on an opportunity. I've always felt like I wanted to do something to make that up to her. There are times when I've tried to talk her into going back to college so she could get her degree. She says it's too late now, but I think she's afraid. I wish she *would* go. I think she'd feel a whole lot better about herself." Although Julie describes her father as a "nice man," she says he was rarely around when she was growing up. He often put in a sixty-hour work week, and he spent little time with his children.

When Ben talks about his father, the description is similar. Ben's father was a hard worker who rarely saw his children.

Ben's mother didn't stay home with the children, either. She resumed her teaching career when Ben was four years old.

"I don't remember that period too well," Ben says the first time we talk about it. "There was a housekeeper who looked after me, but she had a lot of other duties. I know I missed my mother. But I was too young to remember much about it.

"Later on, I remember my dad made fun of my mother for not cooking enough meals. He teased her about all the meetings she had to attend and all the phone calls she took at home. Even though he joked about it, I think Dad was unhappy that she was out of the house so much. A couple of times he got really angry—he'd say 'Where's my dinner?' and so on."

When Julie married Ben, she knew she wanted her life to be much different from her mother's. Julie knew she was capable of continuing to work while she was raising the children. Ben never objected to Julie's continuing her career, but he rarely took the initiative on the home front. Julie remained the primary care-taker: she prepared meals, set up the children's schedules, and stayed home with them when they were sick. Ben's support was always remote.

During one session, Julie complained that she had too many demands on her. Caring for the children, her husband, her career—it was all too much.

Ben responded, "I don't understand what she wants! *What am I supposed to do now?* I do everything she tells me to do."

"It's not what you *do,*" said Julie. "It's your attitude. I'm still the one who's fully responsible."

"I think you're wrong about my attitude. I do feel responsible. You don't appreciate me and how hard I work in this marriage."

—∿—

In therapy, when Julie could talk about how she felt inside, Ben realized there wasn't anything he could "fix" by doing things better or differently.

"I just feel empty inside," Julie said. "I love my children and my home. I still love my work. I should be happy. And I wonder where I missed out. There—I'm beginning to sound like my mother! I guess that's what frightens me most of all. What if I end up being just like her? That's not what I want!"

I asked her to describe how long she'd had that feeling of emptiness. She remembered when she was a little girl playing alone in her room while her father worked. Her mother was downstairs preparing meals. She recalled feeling terribly unloved at that time. She wanted more involvement with her parents, and it wasn't available. She had felt frightened, sad, and lonely—and she cried as she talked about this time of her life.

The frightened, sad, and lonely little girl was still inside her. So my question was, "Julie, can you take care of that little girl? How can you help her—other than by working harder, making more money, and being more efficient? Is there any other way?

"You've been trying to get Ben to take care of that emptiness you describe inside. Do you think he really can?"

Julie looked at Ben. Finally she said, "No, I don't think so."

After that, Ben was able to be more responsive to Julie because he saw her as less of a threat. He didn't see her as someone making demands anymore. He recognized that she was talking about something inside her that he couldn't change.

And Ben was able to talk about some of the feelings of abandonment he'd had as a child. He was angry with me for getting him in touch with those feelings. But it turned out he had very distinct memories of standing by the window after school, looking out and waiting for his mother to come home. He talked about the feelings of loneliness that came back to him.

Ben also started to talk about what was happening in his own life. "I've thrown myself into my work, just like my father did. I'm wondering how much I really want to work. Do you know how confusing that is for me? I don't know whether this is because of what Julie's going through—or maybe it's this therapy. I'm just questioning a lot more things than I did before."

Outwardly, there was little change in Ben, but he seemed to be less robotic and less angry. He recognized the feelings of abandonment that he had when Julie made demands on him or talked about ending the marriage. He also recognized that he couldn't control Julie. Once he gave up trying to control her, he saw that he didn't have to be "doing" all the time.

In an important study of children's relationships to their parents, psychologist Carol Gilligan observed that boys and girls are both emotionally attached to their mothers until they're four or five years old. At that point, a change takes place. The boy has to separate from his mother and he begins to attach more closely to his father. Girls, on the other hand, can remain emotionally connected to their mothers, and they learn from their mothers what it means to be a woman.

As Dr. Gilligan observes, the issues of separation and connectedness stay with us throughout our lives. Deep down, we men have a longing for our mothers because we were separated from them at an early age. But it's shameful to have that longing, because we're men and we're supposed to do what our fathers do. The longing stays inside us, though, and it gets fulfilled for a while when we are married. That's when we reconnect. We have the hallucination that we're whole. But when it turns out that the woman I married has her own life, her own career, her own issues—how do I feel? Abandoned again! My male psyche is desperately hungry. I've already been wounded once, and now it's happening again.

Often, men try to fight the loss by trying to control their mates. "The controlling male" is an archetype that has been identified by the women's movement, and in many respects it's a valid generalization; many men do try to control their wives. But I think the issue of control arises from issues of abandonment: people who are controlling really feel out of control inside.

My father was always the controller in my parent's marriage. Dad was the one who fixed things, who "went to work." As much as possible, he tried to control his spouse, his career, and his children.

When my mother and father were in their mid-seventies, he often nagged her about taking her pills every day.

"Dad, why do you nag her so much?" I asked him once. He replied—and I think honestly—"Because I don't want her to die before me."

Perhaps a younger man could not have admitted that, but at the age of seventy-five, my dad didn't have to pretend to be big and strong. He could admit why he needed to control my mother: *He was afraid of losing her.*

The dynamics are the same for many men, regardless of age. We try to be controllers because of our own abandonment anxiety and our own dependency. If our mates appear needy and dependent, then *we* can appear big and strong and in control.

But male control is a threat to women. A woman who lets herself be controlled is betraying her sisters, her mother, and ultimately herself.

On the surface, the power struggle goes like this:

The man says, "I'm competent to control, and I'll tell you what to do and how to do it."

The woman says, "No, that's not right. I'm going to do it differently."

And that's when male anxiety soars. Because what she's really saying to our psyche is "I can leave you anytime—and I will, if I want to."

But a woman has her needs, too.

Despite the fact that Julie's father was often at work, one thing he did was protect the family. If he was responsible for the income, he was also in charge of allaying anxiety. At the same time, he was less available, and so his daughter did not see his vulnerability as she did her mother's. Like Julie, who wanted to see Ben "without a mask," a woman who wants a man who is strong may also wish for a man who is vulnerable.

My dad never did stop nagging Mom about taking her pills. But she knew that he wasn't doing it because he was trying to control her life. He was doing it because he didn't want her to leave him. After all those years, they still didn't share the same language, but my dad used the only language he had to tell my mom he wanted her to stay around. I never did know whether Mom liked that or not. But every time Dad reminded her to take her pills, I think *he* felt a little bit safer inside.

17

The Impact of Children

❧

I have a fantasy that someone, someday, will create a training school for parents. Allow me to indulge this fantasy for a moment:

The motto over the doorway of this school is an oft-quoted line from the family therapist Carl Whitaker: "To be a good parent, you must enjoy being hated."

As part of the school's curriculum, there are support groups for all parents to help them deal with feelings of helplessness, impatience, and frustration. For men who are about to become fathers, there are courses in "How to Deal with the Loss of a Spouse to an Alien Being," "How to Deal with Feelings of Helplessness Around that Alien Being," and, at the same time, "How to Fall More Deeply in Love than You've Ever Been Before."

For women preparing for motherhood, there is a course called "Pretty Much on Your Own," which gives them permission to talk every day about the upsetting and remarkable changes their bodies are going through. This course is followed by one-on-one counseling around the tough question "Career and/or Family—Does Anyone Have It All?" Finally, every woman can take a special seminar about dealing with her husband after the baby is born.

At the end of the semester, there is a husband-and-wife discussion group entitled "Let's Hold on Tight Because the Ride Is Scary, Bumpy, Exhilarating, and Very Brief, and Ideally We'll Be Holding on Tight When the First Part of the Ride Is All Over, about Eighteen Years from Now."

Of course, this is only a fantasy, because birth, like death, can never be fully prepared for.

A very dear friend of mine who is a therapist gave birth to a beautiful red-haired boy. She refers to him as "my little guy." When she talked about the impact of this child on her husband, she said, "You know, men suffer postpartum depressions, too." Her husband ("A man who never gets sick") had flu symptoms every weekend for the first month after the baby was born. When they talked about it, she found out that he was feeling abandoned. He felt as if his wife had another man because she was spending so much time with the baby. Her husband wanted something for himself.

I told her that many husbands have affairs at this point in their marriage.

"My husband's not that kind of guy," she said. "He just gets sick."

Having a child is a trauma in a marriage. If the marriage is basically intact when the child comes, then a child can be exciting and exhilarating. But a child can also damage a marriage.

In a good marriage, a husband will appreciate his wife's intimacy with their baby—and his wife will want her husband to feel a similar bond of intimacy with their child. They will trust each other completely with the baby. In addition, however, they will maintain their own level of intimacy and see that it is a priority rather than a secondary matter.

In a marriage with problems, there's jealousy and mistrust. The baby often represents a woman's opportunity to be emotionally closer to her child than she is to her husband. And the husband often feels victimized and abandoned by his wife's new-formed intimacy. He therefore has affairs, or invests more in work, or does both.

Gail and Jeff started seeing me when their son, Colin, was nine months old.

The young couple, both twenty-four, came into therapy because they felt that their marriage was deteriorating. Communication had broken down.

Developmentally speaking, they were in an early stage of their marriage when Colin was born. Until the baby came along, Jeff saw Gail as a woman who met all his needs. She was happy with her own career, and she made Jeff feel fulfilled as a man— perhaps for the first time in his life. From her point of view, Gail saw Jeff as the father she'd never had and always wanted; he was reliable, didn't drink, and didn't have affairs. He was loving and attentive to her. In short, neither one knew who the other one really was. They just had their images of each other.

When their son was born, their relationship was put to the test. Both Jeff and Gail had been expecting Gail to be the perfect mother, to maintain her career, and also to be the ideal wife. But it didn't work out that way. She focused on the baby, and whatever energy she had left over went into professional activities. Jeff felt that Gail had deserted him, and he in turn began to seem very remote to her.

"It's as if Jeff just checked out," Gail insisted. "He hardly ever tries to help with the baby—in fact, he's not home very much, and when he is home, he just watches TV. I'm exhausted and desperately need help, and he's not there."

Jeff described how he felt when the baby came along: "I was never so happy in my life as when I first saw Colin. I saw my son as somebody I could be truly intimate with. I wanted to help Gail and be involved with my new family."

Jeff felt both abandoned and frustrated, and he acknowledged that he was also feeling somewhat depressed. He said, "At least if she was sexual in bed, I could tolerate the losses during the day."

"I just don't feel like it," she said. "I don't feel attractive and to be honest I don't feel loved."

I had them face each other and talk about what their complaints really were. Because what they had been doing was expressing their anger at each other to me in a very "reasonable" and modulated way—using words like *frustration* and *sadness*.

I asked Gail to look at Jeff and say, "I'm furious at you because…" And Gail completed the sentence, "… because I feel frightened for the first time. I'm not confident with what I'm doing with this baby. And I need help—I need you—and you're not there. You're not the ideal father I thought you were before Colin came."

I had Jeff complete the same sentence: "I'm furious at you because…" And he completed it with ". . . because, before Colin came along, I got more nurturing from you than I'd ever received in my whole life. And now I'm in a position where I'm jealous of my own son. Not only do I feel abandoned but I'm actually embarrassed. And I'm furious at you for setting up that kind of situation."

Once they got past the anger and were able to acknowledge it, then they were able to talk about their hurt and fear. Both of them lost an ideal parent when Colin was born—when each of them discovered that he was married to a real human being. It was a shocking realization! Both of them needed each other and felt that they lost their best friend. And neither had been able to acknowledge it.

For most of us, our only source of training in how to be a parent comes from the family we grew up in. That could be good news or bad news, of course. If our family's portrait of the world was painted in two colors and we're now trying to paint with a full palette, parenting is going to be a frustrating experience.

Our images of "mother" and "father" usually come from our experiences with our own mothers and fathers. They were the first adults we encountered; throughout childhood they represented most of what adulthood meant to us. And often, I think, we need our own children to re-create and improve our childhood and our spouse to improve on the parenting we received.

But how much can we, as adults, really "improve ourselves" as parents? The famed British psychoanalyst D. W. Winnicott coined the phrase "Good-Enough Mother," suggesting that if we just had mothers who were *good enough*—by no means ideal or perfect—there wouldn't be any serious emotional illness.

I think the same holds true with fathers. No man can hope to be the perfect masculine role model or the ideal example of fatherhood. But if we can tolerate being "good enough," the journey through parenthood will be a more pleasurable one.

Shortly after Gail and Jeff ended their therapy, they wrote to me and said they were going to have another baby. The second baby didn't seem to traumatize the marriage. They tell me they have both enjoyed watching each other be less-than-perfect parents all over again.

We are, perhaps, easily intimidated by the magnitude of parenting. But if we become too impressed by the weightiness of our obligations and responsibilities, there's a chance that we may forget what we most valued in our own parents when we were children.

As my colleague Ed Monte observed, "There are too many parents who forget to play."

We *can* have a sense of play; it *is* allowed, even if we are adults. Even if our own parents were weighed down with work, home, and raising kids, is that how we want *our* children to view adulthood? Do we want them to learn that adulthood means working nineteen-hour days—and that's all? Do we want them to view adults as anxiety-ridden and controlling?

There's a Zen saying that I'm fond of: "Our teachers come from strange places." Our children are our teachers, especially in infancy. They teach us how to deal with feelings of incompetence, impotence, helplessness, confusion, frustration, joy, excitement, and tenderness—the likes of which I have never seen before and may never see again.

And perhaps while they're teaching us, we can teach them that the world of adulthood can also mean pleasure and fun. I would hope that our children find themselves among adults who relish change in their children and change in themselves, who permit themselves to enjoy the unpredictable, the unforeseen, to relish the transformations that we constantly see in the world around us. But perhaps most of all, I would hope that our children discover that adults can be at peace with just being "good enough"—and that those adults are willing to admit they're imperfect, especially in the presence of the children they love.

18

When Divorce Seems the Answer

∾

I want to tell a story about two individuals in the Institute of Marriage.

To some people, this institute is a place to grow and to be creative, a place to love and be loved. To others it's a place to feel stifled, angry, and deathlike. But the externals of that institute are much the same for everyone. Within its home-like walls, people are quartered closely together; doors are sometimes locked, sometimes open; meals and recreation are shared; and those with privileges are free to move about as they wish.

Now imagine that a couple—call them Stuart and Linda—have adjacent rooms in the institute. There's a thin wall between their living quarters. When they first moved in, they were delighted to be living alongside each other. They talked frequently, they passed notes back and forth, and sometimes they both leaned on their respective windowsills gazing up into the starry night.

Then something happened. Today, neither of them can remember what it was. At this point, the actual episode doesn't matter. For whatever reason, Stuart stopped talking about what was in his heart to Linda—and vice versa. The conversation was confined to other subjects, such as the children, the bills, the weekly schedules and appointments.

The means of communication they now maintain would seem very strange to an outsider, even though Linda and Stuart understand perfectly. Each is attuned to the slightest nuance in the other's behavior. When Stuart makes noise in the middle of the night, Linda—on the other side of the thin wall—turns over and sighs, expressing her annoyance. Stuart hears her sigh: for just an instant, he wishes the sigh meant she longed for him, that they were together in bed, holding each other close. But the next instant, his rage and emptiness return. Linda, lying awake, feels her emptiness and still feels very much part of Stuart. But at this point in her life, that connection—instead of feeling loving—feels suffocating.

And so it goes. In all their movements, each gets some response from the other, as though they were doing a dance that neither knew how to change. In a thousand ways, every day, they are in touch with each other. But it is all in signals, all in code—and none of those signals provides comfort.

And there's one more element to this story. When Linda and Stuart were married, they gave each other the keys to their own hearts, assuming that their mate would keep those keys safe. But that didn't happen. Now they have both lost the keys to their own hearts, and they have not yet discovered how to reclaim them.

Ideally, they can reclaim those keys—ideally, they will discover that they are responsible for maintaining those keys themselves.

The most painful session I ever had in my life was with a couple who had decided to separate. Nancy and Jim had a three-year-old daughter, Patricia, and Nancy was eight months pregnant. The parents had not informed Patricia of their plans. Because they were both frightened and didn't know how to tell the daughter, I asked them to bring her in. Patricia brought her baby doll, dressed in diapers and a blue T-shirt. She played quietly while we talked.

During the course of the session, Jim said to Patricia, "Honey, you know Mommy and Daddy haven't been getting along."

His daughter didn't say anything. She went on playing with her doll.

Jim continued, "You know, Mommy and I aren't really friends with each other anymore."

Patricia still didn't say anything.

And he said, "Honey, because of that, Daddy's going to move out."

Patricia put down her doll and turned it to him, and her eyes welled up with tears. She screamed, "Don't leave me, Daddy! Don't do this! Please don't leave me!"

At this point, all four of us in the room wept openly.

The divorce rate in this country has hovered between 40 and 50 percent ever since the 1980s. Millions of families have been and will continue to be affected by the social changes that have come about as a result of the frequency of divorce.

Being a family therapist can be marvelously humbling when we encounter the tide of social forces beyond our control. The pill, the sexual revolution, drugs, war, women's liberation, gay liberation—all have influenced the shape of family structures. Therapists try to measure the changes: we talk about protecting children; we interpret the changes in family lives; and we try to accustom our clients and patients to the shock waves of change. But when we are honest with ourselves, we must admit that these social issues have a profound impact not just on the structure of the family but on the way we as individuals see ourselves, our world, and our relationships.

And yet, in the midst of these fundamental changes in families, we still hear the issues repeated. And we listen to Stuart and Linda—husbands and wives, ex-husbands and ex-wives— sending inarticulate signals of anguish and rage through paper-thin walls:

After fifteen years of marriage, Maggie informed her husband she was not planning to go with him when he went to California on his sabbatical. That message got through: he understood, at last, that his wife believed the marriage was finished. Now he is back in town, but he has not been in touch with her or the children. And he refuses to send any money for the family's support.

Jay is the grown son of parents who have spent the better portion of the past three years working out their divorce arrangements. They had been married for thirty-three years. Jay is trying to maintain an individual relationship with each of them, and he refuses to allow one parent to "dump on" the other in his presence. Whether they choose to stay together bound in their rage to each other, or whether they succeed in working through their divorce, he hopes they will be happier than they are now. But for the last three years, his parents have argued daily about the settlement of their money and property. At one point they had worked out an agreement, they sat down to sign the papers—but then both refused to sign.

—∞—

When Julie initiated the separation from Carl, she was certain that she didn't want to live with him anymore. They'd had furious arguments. Each time, Carl had promised to change but ended up going back to his "old ways." Julie knew she couldn't take it anymore, and she packed her bags and moved out. After the move, her first feeling was relief.

Then another woman moved in with Carl. "I was so angry I couldn't function," says Julie. "I initiated the separation. I wanted it all along. Why am I so angry? Being angry at him seems like such a dead end."

The couple in my office hate each other. In their looks, their conversation, their interaction, they are unremittingly nasty to each other. Both of them talk about their "bad marriage"—but after eighteen years in that marriage, they seem unwilling to end it. Why? What keeps them together?

I ask the woman, "Why do you stay in this marriage? What do you like about him?"

She thinks to herself for a long moment before she replies, "Well, I like his smell."

What she's talking about is a special kind of acceptance that defies explanation. There's so much she hates about her husband, but there are also elements of this marriage that feel comfortable, that make her feel that the marriage belongs to her. So she rails against what she cannot change, yet accepts that this is the hand she's been dealt in life.

Few things are as painful as the decision to end a marriage. Perhaps the only equivalent, in emotional cost, is staying in a bad marriage when both partners have given up hope of ever making it better.

How can we alleviate the pain? *Is* divorce the answer? Is divorce the *only* answer? Is it the answer we *want?* And if we do accept divorce as the "answer" most likely to work, what lies ahead of us?

As always, it is the therapist's prerogative to answer questions with questions. These, then, are mine:

"Have you been able to hear your spouse, without feeling attacked? Has your spouse been able to talk about his or her pain and the other feelings that underlie the anger and silence? Have you had the courage to talk to your mate about what's going on in your heart— without holding that person responsible for fixing it?"

Like Stuart and Linda, the couple in the story, we may be holding the keys to each other's room. But are we just sending signals—slamming doors, grumbling, sighing—using an unintelligible and mysterious vocabulary to articulate the anguish inside us?

"Do you want to change your partner—or to change yourself?"

It is nearly always impossible to change our partners. It is possible to change ourselves if we are in pain and we *want* to change. But we do not automatically change ourselves by getting divorced, any more than we change ourselves by beginning a relationship or getting married.

"If you could wave your magic wand and create the perfect marriage, what would it look like?"

I ask this question because every marriage is imperfect. And the next question is, How much imperfection are you willing to tolerate? If we can recognize the "ideal marriage" that we carry around in our heads (along with the images of "ideal mate," "ideal parent," and "ideal *me*"), perhaps we can acknowledge the ways in which that marriage is unattainable.

"Can you protect your children's childhood?"

When children become conduits of their parents' rage (parents who are married, as well as those who are separated or divorced), those children lose the privilege of living out their childhood. Can we direct our rage toward the adult who is the object of our feelings and allow our children to become adults in their own time? Or, ideally, can we acknowledge the pain, abandonment, and helplessness that are behind our rage?

"Do you want to end the marriage—or to begin it over again?"

It is sad to have lost the person we married—a person who was, perhaps, far more passionate, carefree, attentive, and romantic than the person we live with now. Can we accept the person who has taken the place of the mate we once knew? Can we let go of the person we married—who was, after all, partly an illusion—and find value in the person who now shares our home?

For about half the married people reading this book, divorce is a likely alternative: at some point, it will represent the answer to whatever problems or issues have arisen in the marriage. Perhaps a divorce will be the first step toward a more fulfilling and satisfying relationship with someone else. It may even be a *necessary* step in our growth as human beings. It may be a way to assert and protect the integrity of our selves and our values. And for our children, divorce may be the means of protecting them from a spouse who endangers their health or well-being.

But divorce is really only the first step in the separation process. The separation is not complete until we have also let go of the grief, the pain, and the rage that we carry within us.

I'm reminded of a woman who called in to *Voices in the Family* some years ago, asking about the impact of divorce on teenage children. She described with anger how her ex-husband had walked out on her and her teenage sons without any warning. Now this woman was concerned about the way this had affected the boys' lives, and she was angry at her ex-husband for his irresponsibility. Clearly, she wanted me to agree with her and confirm that the man who walked out on her had behaved irresponsibly.

I asked, "When did he walk out?"

"Fifteen years ago," she replied, adding, "Of course, he's been dead for eight years now."

I was very much saddened by the fact that this woman not only carried her anger at her husband to *his* grave but would probably carry it to *her* grave as well.

Yes, sometimes divorce does seem to be the answer. But when that's the case, what I wish for everyone is that the separation be clean—that it be final—that we can grieve the death that the loss of any marriage really is.

In a very fundamental and profound way, a part of us dies when a marriage dies. And if we don't grieve that death within us, then in all likelihood we're doomed to repeat the problems that came up in our first marriage. If we try to hold on to the partner whom we are also trying to give up, we may continue to carry the anger and the feeling of victimization into the next marriage, into the next relationship, or for the rest of our lives. It's only through healthy grief and mourning that we can get past those feelings and open the door for healthier relationships in our future.

What I wish for all of us is to find a safe place inside, where we are able to acknowledge what's in our hearts. If we can share what's in our hearts with our mate, the marriage will be a safe place. If we cannot—if the marriage must end—then we must let go of the part that has died and hope to find a place in ourselves that feels safe. Not a place where we're taken care of. Just a safe place.

19

As a Marriage Matures

ↂ

Some years ago I was treating two couples. in each case the man had broken his neck and was a quadriplegic.

One couple had been married six months when the accident happened. I saw them on Tuesdays in my office.

The other marriage was in its forty-first year. I went to visit the couple each Thursday in West Philadelphia.

Broad-shouldered, square-jawed Russ had been finishing up his training at the state police academy when a fall from a three-story ladder put an end to his career plans. His wife, Nancy, was an attractive twenty-two-year-old woman who looked as if she had just lived through a nightmare. She appeared tired, angry, and preoccupied.

Russ had been near the top of his class in the academy and certain of graduation. During the short time he and Nancy had been married, they had carefully charted their plans for the future. After Russ passed his exam and became a state trooper, they would have been in a position to buy their first home and begin a family. Nancy had been doing unsatisfying clerical work while Russ was in the academy, and she had looked forward to quitting her job as soon as that was financially possible.

Nancy's family lived in the Midwest. Before the accident, the whole family had planned to come east for Russ's graduation, and Nancy had made extensive arrangements for their visit. After the accident, when Russ was in the hospital, her mother and father had offered to help out, but Nancy told them she could handle everything, and she had told them not to come. At her insistence, they had cancelled their trip.

Nancy's disappointment at the dashing of her expectations had stirred an anger that she couldn't hide. A lot of her anger was directed toward Russ's family. They surrounded and protected Russ, taking care of all his physical necessities without involving Nancy. Blocked by the family, she felt very abandoned and unprotected. Even though she was fiercely independent of her own family, she, too, needed to be taken care of and nurtured. Russ certainly couldn't protect her now, and his family wasn't doing anything for her. So most of her anger was directed at her husband's family, but she also took some of it out on Russ for ignoring her and her needs.

Russ said he resented his own dependency and everybody's being "so damn helpful." He couldn't acknowledge that his wife had needs, too, and he was angry about her complaining: "After all, look what I'm living through. How can I worry about you?"

For ten months, Russ and Nancy and I worked as hard as we could, and in the end we had to conclude that the marriage was doomed. There was not enough commitment and not enough history and too much anger in the room.

Neither Russ nor Nancy was making any discoveries about the other. Neither wanted to explore the changes that the other human being was going through. Having lost the marriage that they had planned, they couldn't imagine any other kind. And they couldn't let go of the dream of a life that was now unavailable to them.

They were divorced within a year.

On Thursdays I drove into West Philadelphia and parked my van in front of a small, two-story row-house. There was an electric wheelchair lift up to the front porch.

Inside, the house was dark, close, and crowded with worn furnishings. The antiseptic smell of alcohol hung in the air. The narrow dining room had been made over into a bedroom. The wheelchair and TV were in the same room. This was where Barry spent much of his time. Miriam slept in a room upstairs on the second floor.

This couple had been referred to me by Magee Rehabilitation Center in Philadelphia. Barry had broken his neck in an on-the-job heavy machinery accident, and he had been treated at the center. The therapists at Magee were concerned about how he would readjust after returning to his home.

This couple was living in the center of a West Philadelphia neighborhood wracked with poverty. The streets were littered with broken glass; drug dealing went on around the corner. The couple themselves had no money, yet their relationship was rich.

To Miriam and Barry, a broken neck was just another event in their forty-one years of living together. Their main question was, What changes were necessary in order for them to adjust to this new event in their lives?

They had to teach me how to treat them. I was used to dealing with problematic relationships. With this couple I had to spend the first two sessions just understanding what their needs were. And while I listened to Miriam and Barry talk to each other, the darkness in the house dissipated. There was much tenderness and much love; their relationship glowed.

Finally, they helped me hear what the issues were. They wanted to know whether they could still make love—and how? Would he be hurt physically? Miriam needed "permission" to go out shopping by herself or with her friends, leaving Barry alone in the house. Would he be all right while she was gone? Barry still dreamed of going to shopping malls and visiting his friends in Baltimore. Was that something a quadriplegic could do?

I saw them for ten sessions, and we developed a warm, tender relationship. That was all they needed. When we ended therapy, I felt a deep regret—because I had enjoyed being with them.

When a marriage matures and you have a history together, things usually feel safer. It's safer to argue, safer to disagree. Ideally, as the marriage goes on, you love the *person* and not just the feeling of love or the comfort of being in love. And ideally, you don't want to alter that person. You do not want to make your mate healthier, happier, less depressed; nor do you want to add anything or take anything away from the person you married.

And you can tolerate differences in each other. If she's social and he's a couch potato, it's okay for her to go out socially and for him to be home watching the ballgame. Each is happy that the other is having a good time, and neither resents the other.

That's generous love. (Selfish love is when she drags him out or he keeps her home. But that's not really love: that's control.)

It takes generous love to survive the large and small events of a long relationship. It takes generous love to keep on listening to each other—and to *learn* from each other.

In Jewish tradition, anyone who would become a rabbi is told, "First, you must be a servant." In my teaching I tell my students, "Never stop being a student."

We never, ever know our mates. We can never assume that we know who they are or what they're thinking, because we never fully understand them. Our mates, like all human beings, are dynamic and ever-changing.

And so are we. When you reread a classic or see a movie that you saw years ago, does it seem different? *It* hasn't changed; it's *you* who have changed. Your eyes are different. Your mind is different. Your dynamic has changed.

In a marriage that's forty years old, you can ask your mate, "How do you feel about retiring?" or "Do you miss the children as much as I do?" or "Who have been our closest friends for forty years?"—questions you couldn't ask earlier in the relationship because the questions didn't have any meaning back then. Your relationship was younger then; you shared less history. You didn't have the data or the concern about those questions. But now the issues have become relevant, interesting, important.

In a marriage that's forty years old, you can ask your mate, "How would you like to make love now? What can we do differently? What else can we explore?"

It takes one and a half lifetimes to understand your mate. Your tastes change. Your life changes. Your view of the world changes. Your feelings about your own life and death change. But you can never stop becoming a student.

And when your mate says that he or she *knows* how you feel, you owe it to yourself and your marriage to say, "No, you don't." And then tell your mate how you *do* feel. Because if your marriage is alive, your mate is a student of you as well.

20

Making Peace with Our Mates

∾

During the first ten years of our marriage, Sandy and I struggled with what most other couples struggle with. How much intimacy were we going to be comfortable with? How much intimacy did I require, and how much did she require? How much could she and I tolerate, and how much did we need? Of course, the formula was ever in flux, as I think it is in all marriages.

In our marriage I was usually "the pursuer" in the relationship—that is, I was the one "in charge" of going after intimacy, while Sandy was "in charge" of setting the limits and boundaries. (In most marriages I've observed, it's the opposite. Generally, it's the woman who is the pursuer, and the man who is in charge of the limits.)

That was in the first ten years.

Then I had my accident, and during the first eighteen months after the accident, Sandy was with me every day in the hospital. I felt more bonded with her than I had with any other human being any other time in my life. Sandy knew all the details of what was going on in every part of my body. When I got a urinary tract infection, she wept. She watched when the nurses changed my catheter. (Because she was trained in the procedure, she was watching for mistakes.) When I had surgery for skin breakdown, her face showed that she felt the physical pain that I couldn't feel.

I felt she knew me completely. That was my delusion.

One day, Sandy was sitting in a chair near my bedside and we were talking. I could see that she had a question that she was having difficulty formulating. I encouraged her.

When she finally asked the question, her eyes were filled with tears.

"How does it feel?" she asked.

"How does what feel?"

"How does it feel not to feel?"

She was frightened and embarrassed. Her pain was visible. She wanted to understand something about me that would forever be beyond her comprehension.

This time I wept, because I saw that the feeling of being bonded and being fully understood by Sandy was a myth. *Ideally,* I wanted to be known at the level where I would be connected and intimate. All of us need and want to be known at such a level—but only in infancy is that need realized. The need inside me would never be met.

I could not say that Sandy was inadequate to fill that need inside me. She didn't cause that need, and it certainly could not have been cured by her. I had to make peace with the fact that my need to be fully known would never be fulfilled by anyone.

I struggled with that notion for months. And when I could finally give up my delusions about the person with whom I was most intimate, only then could I face Sandy differently. I was able to see her not as a caretaker or mother or some kind of ideal being that could fully know me—I saw her as just a woman with the same human flaws and frailties that I had.

It has been said that we all have a need to be known that exceeds our need to be loved. That's a human condition. But it's also a human condition that we can never be fully known in that way. Part of what goes on in marriage is that we may get angry at the other person for not knowing us. But with maturity, we give up insisting that our spouse fully know what goes on inside us.

Alex and Janice, a childless couple in their mid-sixties, had been married for forty years when they first came in for treatment. Alex was furious and intolerant. He was thinking of leaving the marriage.

Alex's mother had been depressed; so had Janice's; and each had lived some of the roles they had learned from parents in their family of origin. When Janice went through periodic depression, Alex became Janice's caretaker and protector, as he had for his mother.

Janice felt terribly guilty; she felt she was less of a person than she "could be" or "should be" for her husband. When she was depressed she would become angry at herself for being inadequate as a human being. Her anger became toxic both to her and to the marriage.

For the first twenty-five years of their marriage, Alex had been very protective of Janice. He had tried to shield her from the stress of life and had given her extra care when she was depressed. Secretly, however, Alex resented Janice—so much so that he'd had an affair and had a lover for years. When he first saw me in therapy, he told me he didn't think there was any way he could survive this marriage unless he continued the love affair.

As we worked in therapy, Janice eventually stopped battling herself to "get past this depression." She was able to give up her anger and acknowledge that having depressive episodes didn't mean that she or her mother was defective; those episodes were just a fact of life. She began to stop blaming herself.

As it turned out, even with all the appropriate treatments, Janice would have to struggle with her depression, off and on, for the rest of her life. But when she gave up the battle to "control" her depression, her episodes became less frequent and less intense. She began to trust herself and her psyche, understanding that she would always have temporary episodes. Through her work in therapy, she discovered ways to blame herself less for her inadequacies as a wife.

Alex had always resented being the one responsible for bringing energy to the marriage. But for forty years he had been with Janice. He'd never left her! Whatever his reasons, despite what his wife had and what she didn't have, Alex loved her. He was getting something out of the marriage. Now he was finally able to see and understand that his wife's depression was part of the package. He recognized that she would never be the active one in their social life; she would never bring more energy to the marriage. But once Alex was able to give up the delusion that Janice would "stop being depressed," he was finally able to see her as she was.

The last time Janice and Alex came to see me, they were more at peace with themselves and each other and their marriage was far more comfortable and nurturing. They were looking forward to a future together. Alex knew that when Janice was depressed, he would need to get involved with himself and do things that made him feel good. And Janice understood that her depressions were temporary. They were able to enjoy themselves and each other, knowing that theirs was an imperfect marriage, but a marriage with a lot of love. They had made peace with the imperfect marriage rather than battling to make it more perfect.

And Alex's love affair?

He never made a conscious decision to give up his lover. But it happened anyway—slowly, over the course of therapy. First he stopped having a sexual relationship with the woman he was seeing. Then he saw her less frequently. When therapy ended, he had not seen her socially in six months. There was no official ending. But as his needs diminished, as he began to make peace with his marriage and his life, he must have felt less need for a lover.

I don't see how we can begin to make peace with anybody unless we begin to understand something important about life: that it's fraught with imperfections. Bodies have warts and wrinkles; so do personalities, and so do relationships. Some bodies are three-quarters paralyzed. Some personalities are three-quarters paralyzed.

If we can accept these facts of life—if we have the abilities, the skills, the strength, and the wisdom to accept them—then we are in a position to make peace.

There's another aspect to making peace with our mate.

I recall talking with a woman who was married to a man with bipolar disorder. She never knew, day by day, hour by hour, when he would be "up" and when he'd be "down." Their relationship went through numerous blowups, but the woman had stayed with her husband through it all.

I asked her how she could make peace with her husband.

She told me, "I've fallen in love with his core."

What she loved was not his behavior. She didn't love the volatility in the relationship—in fact, she actually disliked it. But she had fallen in love with this man's soul. Their relationship was spiritual. With this man she felt lovable and therefore loved. Though her husband's behavior might never change, she could acknowledge and accept his imperfections and still love his core.

∾

PART THREE

Our Children

21

Listening to Our Children

∾

The following conversation occurred during a live broadcast of my radio show. My caller was an eleven-year-old girl. This is a nearly complete transcript of our conversation, omitting only the suggestions I gave her at the very end:

GIRL (*sounding very nervous and hesitant*): I want to know what uses you can make of a psychiatrist if you don't really want to go to him.

ME (*supposedly an authority, totally baffled by this question*): Boy—I really don't know. Are you going to one?

GIRL: Yes. I mean, instead of just like sitting there and not really having anything to say—like, what could you . . .

ME (*realizing this will take some time*): All right. Let's think this out together. How come you're going?

GIRL: Because my mom wants me to, and she thinks that it's good for the family.

ME (*not sure what's going on here; noncommittally, without asking a question or making a statement*): She thinks it's good for the family.

GIRL: Yes.

ME: Do you know why—what's the problem with the family?

GIRL: Well, I guess she thinks we could just be a little better.

ME: The family could be a little better. . . Is your whole family going?

GIRL: Well, we only have two people, but, um, we're both going together.

ME: The two people are you and your mom?

GIRL: Yeah.

ME: Okay, let's do it this way. If this psychiatrist could change something with the wave of a magic wand, what would he do for you? And what would he do for your mom?

GIRL: I guess . . . we wouldn't argue so much.

ME: You and your mom wouldn't argue?

GIRL: Yeah.

ME: What do you argue about?

GIRL: Well, just, like, stupid things sometimes. Like, we can't really talk it over, I guess.

ME: Do you know why you argue with your mom and she argues with you? Are you angry at each other?

GIRL: Maybe a little bit.

ME: What are you angry at her for?

GIRL: I don't know . . . I guess . . . I don't know.

ME: All right. Where's your dad?

GIRL: I see him every other weekend. But my mom and dad are divorced.

ME: When did they divorce?

GIRL: When I was a baby.

ME: How old are you now?

GIRL: I'm eleven.

ME: Oh, a long time ago.

GIRL: Yeah.

ME: Do you know what your mom's angry at you for?

GIRL: She just wants it to be like—she doesn't want us to argue so much, and she wants to, like, not argue about little things—

ME: Okay.

GIRL: —and be able to talk about them.

ME: Okay. You already answered part of your first question—the question about "if you don't want to go, what can you get out of it." Now, what you told me is that one thing you *want* to get out of it is that you won't want to argue with your mom so much. And you don't want her to argue so much with you. Do you think your mom understands you?

GIRL: Yeah.

ME: She *does* understand you—she understands what goes on inside you?

GIRL: Most of the time, I guess so.

ME: Boy—you're one lucky eleven-year-old. That doesn't go on with many eleven-year-olds.

GIRL: (*Laughs*)

ME: All right, now. I said, "If the psychiatrist had a magic wand . . . " And you said what he would do is make it so you guys would argue less.

GIRL: Yeah.

ME: Now, picture this. He's got the magic wand. And he's going to reach over and hand *you* the magic wand. Now what are you going to do? It's in *your* hands. What are you going to do?

GIRL: Try to talk things over with her when we have an argument.

ME: What do you want to talk about? How do you want to do it differently?

GIRL: Um—just not start yelling. But just sit down and talk about it.

ME: What kinds of things...? This is a toughy—you ready for a toughy?

GIRL: Yeah.

ME: What kinds of things are important to you that never really get talked about well with your mother? Can you tell me what things always seem to start arguments with your mother?

GIRL: Well, what school I'm going to go to next year. And where we're going to move next year. But she has to move somewhere near her medical school.

ME: She does . . . Okay, pick one of those.

GIRL: Um . . . the moving.

ME: Okay, the moving. What are your feelings about the moving?

GIRL: Well, I want to move somewhere near my friends, like in Germantown, I guess.

ME: And where does she want to move?

GIRL: Near Norristown.

ME: Near Norristown. Okay, what happens if you move away? What happens to you if you lose this argument?

GIRL: I guess I feel pretty bad.

ME: Why? What would you miss? What would you lose?

GIRL: I'd be away from my friends.

ME: Yeah.

GIRL: And I guess I wouldn't be exactly where I wanted to be.

ME: Are you scared about moving?

GIRL (*instantly*): Yeah.

ME: Scared about making new friends—wondering whether you could or not?

GIRL: No, not really.

ME: Okay, what is it you're scared about with the move?

GIRL: Moving away from the friends I already made.

ME: Why does she argue with you about that—do you know?

GIRL: Because she knows she has to move somewhere near her medical school.

ME: Yeah. You said you argue because you're scared inside. Ask your mom why she argues—what goes on inside her?

GIRL (*off the phone—to her mother*): Mom, why do you argue? (*after a moment, to me*): Because she feels guilty.

ME: Oh. Do you know what that means when she says she feels guilty?

GIRL: No.

What a wonderful eleven-year-old—bold enough to call a live radio show, paying attention to all of Dr. Dan's questions, thinking carefully about her answers, and answering honestly. And yet, how difficult to find out what she was feeling—to find her pain, her anger, her unhappiness, her confusion. With my encouragement she was trying hard to get at the issue, but for both of us it was pure detective work.

And look how long it took! It's a lengthy transcript, and I quoted it in full because I have a point to make, and not necessarily one that every parent will like to hear. Listening to children takes time. Sometimes it takes a bit of imagination and fantasy. ("If you had a magic wand, what would you do?") Sometimes, interpretation. ("Okay, you don't want to argue so much. But what do you argue *about*?") Sometimes, you just find yourself saying, "Yeah, okay, I think I understand that part. And now tell me about—"

Listening to children also takes patience. When we become impatient, it's often because we can't tolerate our own helplessness or we can't tolerate listening to a child's misery. We find that we can listen to just so much—and then we try to talk the child out of her pain or show her how to fix it.

I'm sure it was easier for me to be patient with the girl on the phone than it would have been for her mother. After all, it wasn't *my* daughter who was hurting; this girl's misery had nothing to do with what was going on inside me. For the parent listening to his own child, what happens inside is different. We may wonder, Is it our pain that is causing the child's misery? Is there something we *could* do, that we *aren't* doing, to make things right for him? When we're being impatient with children, what we usually have to do is separate ourselves from our own pain. Generally that pain involves helplessness. If we can tolerate our helplessness, we can usually listen when our children talk.

Toward the end of my conversation with the girl, I asked her to ask her mother why *she* argued. And her mother told her daughter, "Because I feel guilty."

The cliché about guilt is that it "ties us in knots." But there's something else guilt does: it creates *noise* in our heads. And when our own guilt, our own angst, is creating so much noise inside, how can we just sit back and listen? There have been times when the noise inside my own head was so loud it was like a pair of sneakers banging around inside a dryer.

At the end of that eleven-year-old's call, I suggested that after she got off the phone she might ask her mother to explain what it meant when she said she "felt guilty." By explaining it, her mother wouldn't "cure" her guilt or make it go away. But if this girl's mother could talk about her guilt, she might then be in a better position to *listen* to her daughter.

And that's what I think we owe our children and ourselves. When that old sneaker is banging around inside our heads—we can try to be aware of the noise and *not* try to compensate for it. If we can first acknowledge to ourselves and our kids that we're too consumed by our own "noise," then we might be more able to listen.

As parents, we want to provide a safe environment for our children. But we can't do that unless we feel safe, unless we feel at peace. Not an "existential" peace—just peace for a moment, so the noise in our head stops for a little while.

I recall when my daughter Ali, at the age of eight, was embroiled in various battles with kids at the bus stop. She was being teased every morning, and the more she tried to defend herself, the worse it got. When she started to tell me what was going on, I couldn't stand it. Those kids were picking on *my* precious little girl! She was scared, she was in pain—and all I wanted to do was make sure it never happened again. So I told her what to do about it, how to make those kids stop picking on her. And *nothing* I said was comforting to her! The more I told her how she could fix it, the more miserable and scared she felt.

She didn't want my *advice*. She just wanted to be heard. Her message to me was, "Please, Dad, just listen to what I'm going through." And I was so anxious and protective that I couldn't give her what she needed.

Had I been able to listen, then I could have said, "Ali, do you want some advice?"

If she did want advice, I could have allowed her to say so. That would have empowered her: she would have been getting my advice because she asked for it, not because I thought it was good for her or thought she should hear it.

What can a parent say to a child who's in a situation like this and is feeling miserable? I think we can offer to intervene, as long as we're truly prepared to allow the child to decline our help. I could have asked Ali whether she wanted me to talk to the kids and at the same time made it clear that I wouldn't do that without her permission. But if I just went out and talked to the kids and told them to stop bothering my daughter, then I'd be doing the same thing the kids were doing—beating her down and making her feel more like a powerless little child.

When we ask a child's permission to help, she is empowered. She can decide what to do for herself, and, in addition, she can decide whether she wants us to intervene on her behalf.

But no matter what we offer, no matter what we would like to do for our children, in the end we might just have to tolerate the child's misery. Children do get miserable, and we can't fix it. That's part of their growing up. As long as the children are not in real danger, more often than not we just have to trust that they've got the resources to work the problem out. And we can let them know that we trust them to find a way.

The kids who come into my office with their families complain most about the fact that "no one listens." Ideally, as parents we hope to provide a safe environment where kids can talk about their feelings without being advised or reprimanded or told what to do. But that means we have to steer them away from our own anxiety—and to do that we have to try, if we can, to stop the noise in our own heads.

You don't have to be a kid chronologically to feel you're not being heard. Jeanette, a forty-year-old patient of mine, recently divorced, was having a difficult time of it. She was often depressed. She was wondering where her support systems were. Whom could she trust, and how much?

I asked her, "Could you call your mother?"

She thought a moment and shook her head.

"I don't think I can," she said. "My mother can't hear my heart."

I found her statement very poignant. At forty, Jeanette was afraid that her mother would give her advice, tell her what to do and how to feel better, that her mother would get anxious, that she couldn't tolerate her daughter's feelings.

Often Jeanette's words would come back to me; I think they're at the core of what all of us want to do with our children. We want to hear their hearts. And much of what we do with them is just clearing the way to make that happen.

Young children don't know how to say to their parents, "Hey, you're not listening." If the parent isn't listening, the child's experience of that is likely to be "There's something wrong with what I'm saying," or "There must be something wrong with me," or "What I'm saying isn't valuable," or "*I'm* not valuable." That's why it's so important for a parent to be able to say (if it's the case), "I can't hear you right now. I'm too upset. Can we talk about this later?"

Once we've said that to a child, how do we make ourselves available again?

Oftentimes, just *saying* we're upset is enough to clear out our ears so we're able to hear. If the child is old enough—and generally, that's about ten years old—he's likely to ask why we're feeling upset. Then we might say why we're anxious, overwhelmed, or depressed; and once we tell them why, we're more available to hear them.

If we *can't* hear them right away, it's important to get back to them. If we said we would listen to them later, but don't, then we're lying to our children. More often than not, they'll come back to us and remind us that we promised to talk with them. But if they don't, it's our responsibility to give them another chance to talk about themselves.

What if a child's words "push your buttons"? What if you simply can't tolerate what the child is trying to tell you?

In the short run, you might bring in your spouse to support you or help you with the child. But in the long run, we want our children to be able to talk to both their parents. So we need to recognize that their words are painful to us—so painful that we can't listen. And if that's the case, we know there's some important learning we can do about ourselves. When we truly can't listen, when it's just too painful for us much of the time, it may be a good idea to begin therapy.

When what a child says makes us feel intolerably hurt or guilty, it's an opportunity to liberate ourselves. Not through the child, but through learning what that guilt and pain are all about. If you can't hear your child, then you're carrying a burden that you can be liberated from; you're feeling a pain you don't need.

At one extreme, a young child's experience of a parent's not listening is that he feels invisible; he feels that he does not or should not exist. At the other extreme is a child who is likely to feel safer, feel more valuable, just because someone can hear his heart. And we feel more valuable and more real if we are able to hear that child.

22

What Do We Expect of Our Children?

∾

I'm sure all of us had a Mrs. Mcnesbit sometime when we were in elementary school.

Mrs. McNesbit was my fourth-grade teacher. And I was scared to death of her. She rearranged the seating in the class-room every week on the basis of how each of her students had done the previous week. If you were currently at the top of the class, you got to sit in the first seat in the first row. If you rated second, you got the second seat, and so on, all the way to the back row. And if you happened to be the worst student in the class, you got the very last seat all the way over at the end of the very last row.

Now, in fourth grade I was a very unpredictable student. During the year, my class position ranged all the way from first seat, first row, to last seat, last row. I was always trying pretty hard, but I never knew when I'd end up doing well—or terribly. As it turned out, by the end of the year, I was in the last seat in the second row, in the sixtieth percentile. But fourth grade was the most painful year I ever had in school.

I continued to struggle with poor academic performance right up through high school. I had difficulty getting into college, and once I was in, I had difficulty staying there. It is a painful legacy that I still carry.

Many years later I discovered I had a learning disability that helped to explain why my progress was so erratic. By the time I found out about the disability, I had also discovered ways to compensate. But the horrible memory of that year with Mrs. McNesbit never faded.

Forward, now, to my daughter's fifth-grade class. Up to this point, Ali had been getting along well in school. But in fifth grade we began getting reports that she was having trouble in class.

And right away, I began to panic internally. Periodically, I got angry at her when she was watching TV instead of doing her homework. I was intolerant of her failure to achieve—and terrified that she would have to walk in my path. What if she flunked out of college? What if she had to carry the shame and pain that I'd carried most of my life?

So when Ali displayed the first hint of having difficulty in school, I overreacted. I panicked. Caught up in my anger, I began to think about everything I'd had to do to compensate for my learning disability. I recalled the early years of my professional life, when I'd worked furiously to prove to myself, to my parents, and to the world that I *could* succeed. I had turned into a workaholic. And finally my body had rebelled. I couldn't keep food down. I had constant intestinal problems, and I put off seeing the doctor until I couldn't deny the state of my health any longer. At the age of twenty-eight I was diagnosed as having a spastic colon. I knew the implications: still a young man, I had the disease of a person twice my age. Something was wrong with the system. I had to take a look at my life and see what was going wrong.

I recalled the day when I received the diagnosis. I was at home. I was in pain. And I recalled the sudden sense of relief. At that point I had realized that I couldn't try any harder; I couldn't push any more. I had realized that perhaps I belonged right where I'd always been, among all those kids in the second row. Those were my kind of kids. And when I realized that, I felt less ashamed of being the "underachiever."

Now, as Ali entered a difficult time in her schooling, I had a choice. Was it fair of me to push her toward overworking, over-compensating, overachieving—and probably, at some point in her life, becoming the kind of workaholic that I had been?

Of course, I didn't want Ali to fail in school, but I didn't want her to become a young woman with the premature illnesses of an aging person, either. Ali had to be free to be Ali. She would have her own struggles and her own shame to deal with. But she would be less likely to carry my legacy if I took responsibility for it on my own.

I think one of the problems with having children is that we're inevitably too young to know who we are when we have them. None of us feels completely whole or completely finished. And how often we wish our children would surpass us, to help us close the gaps in our lives.

I'm reminded of Louise, a patient in her early thirties who had a full-time career and was raising two boys. She said she had always received mixed messages from her mother. Sometimes the message was "Go out, work hard, be successful, have your own life." But now that she had children, she said her mother was always asking, "Are your boys okay? Are you looking after them? Do they have everything they need?"

When Louise's mother, Carla, came in to therapy and talked about herself, Louise began to see why the messages were confusing. All the time Louise was growing up, her mother had held part-time jobs and done occasional volunteer work, but she had never pursued her ambition to become a full-time professional. So, on the one hand, her mother felt that she had never achieved as much as she could have—and on the other, she had always felt guilty about leaving her daughter at home with sitters and housekeepers.

Carla had pushed Louise to be an achiever and to have a career, and she was very proud of her. At the same time, she felt guilty for having the fantasy about her own career, and she needed reassurance that her grandchildren were being cared for. Louise, carrying the legacy of her mother's guilt and her mother's fantasy, was indeed getting mixed messages. And there was nothing *she* could do to resolve her mother's conflicts.

If we're content with ourselves and if our marriage is a loving and respectful one, our children will have room to grow. Of course, that's an ideal concept, because we're never fully content with ourselves and nobody's marriage is perfect. But if we hold on to expectations that our children will take great strides that we've never taken, or fill in the big missing parts of ourselves, then they're likely to be limited in the areas they can explore emotionally.

Our children are affected by the "warts" in our hearts and histories, just as we were deeply affected by those in our parents'. And the extent to which we're not at peace with—not even aware of—our own warts is the extent to which our children will be affected by them.

In one family I treated, an eighteen-year-old girl, Charlene, had been hospitalized for substance abuse. She had performed poorly in school and had been using drugs for almost ten years. Her mother, Frances, was an attorney, and her father was a successful businessman. She had an older brother in medical school and a younger sister who was also doing well.

In one session, the mother and daughter got into an argument. Frances said angrily, "Damn it, why don't you change? Why don't you perform?"

Charlene replied, with tears in her eyes, "I can never be in your league. Why don't you give up? I can *never* please you. I *quit!*"

At this point, they were both tearful.

Later in the session, I asked the daughter, "What is it that you're quitting? What's the contest all about?"

And she said, "I can never get my mother's approval no matter what I do."

Was this issue the "wart" that the mother was carrying? I said to Frances, "Tell me about your relationship with *your* mother."

Frances told me that her mother had always felt trapped in her house and had always complained about being an unfulfilled woman. She was angry in her marriage and angry with her lifestyle. "It felt like Mom was always critical of me," said Frances. "I always dreamed if I could become a professional, I would be doing it for her and she would be happy. But you know what? She's still critical of me, no matter what I do. I still can't get her approval."

And Charlene jumped in, "Because you couldn't get her approval, did you want me to get her approval for you?"

Frances realized that was part of what was going on. The legacy of dissatisfaction with her daughter—really borne of her mother's dissatisfaction with *her*self—had been carried on for another generation. This very successful woman had a gap inside her; she had never received her mother's approval, and she couldn't live without it. She was never able to say, "Well, that's hopeless. I'll have to get my approval elsewhere."

For Charlene, using drugs was an escape from the pain of never having her mother's approval. And the drugs also underscored how different she was from her mother. Because her mother knew about Charlene's substance abuse, she was in pain. And so Charlene had found a way to deflect her mother's disapproval, to escape from her own pain, and to force her mother to admit hers.

With some work in therapy, when Frances was able to give up seeking approval from her mother, she was able to free up her daughter—and Charlene *felt* more free. She was free to be either a success or failure, but more importantly, to be herself. And the mother was better able to hear her daughter's heart.

23

Children and Anger

෴

The case was referred to me by an elementary-school counselor.

Ronnie, a nine-year-old, was getting out of control in the cafeteria and hitting other kids with his lunch tray. Some children had actually been hurt. The counselor had spoken to the family about it, and the parents were concerned, but nothing they did at home improved Ronnie's behavior at school.

I invited the whole family to come in.

Vince, Ronnie's father, was an installer for the telephone company. His wife Andrea was a slim, neat, and attractive woman who came in holding the hands of her daughters, a six-year-old and a four-year-old.

Ronnie was big and stocky for his age. Unlike the rest of the family, who seemed hesitant, he looked around my office curiously, even eagerly. He had trouble sitting still in his seat. He seemed a rough-and-tumble kind of kid, very different from the rest of his family.

After we all got to know each other a bit, I asked Ronnie about his anger.

"Do you know why you hit kids in the cafeteria?" I asked.

"It's just fun," he said, looking me directly in the eye.

"Do you know *why* it's fun?"

"I don't know. It just is."

"Okay. Well, maybe we can figure out why it's fun. But right now, I'd like to talk with your father a little bit. Okay?"

"Sure," said Ronnie.

I started to talk with Vince about his work. Almost immediately, he mentioned his supervisor, whom he described as a hard-headed, extremely unlikable person. At this point, Andrea joined in to say that she thought her husband was very unfairly treated on his job and underpaid besides.

I noted this must be hard. "With three kids in the family, it must be tough to make ends meet." I turned to Vince again. "Do you think you're being fairly paid?"

He shrugged. "I guess so," he said. "I make about the same as everyone else at my level."

"He won't ask for a raise," Andrea put in.

"I could ask, but it wouldn't do any good," said Vince, still looking at me rather than his wife.

"Vince has the worst boss in the whole building," said Andrea to me. "I don't know how he puts up with him every day."

"That must be a pain," I said to Vince.

"Sure is," he agreed.

"Are you angry at your boss?"

"No. There's nothing I can do about it anyway."

I asked Andrea whether she was angry at Vince for not doing anything.

"No," she replied, "I know he's doing the best he can."

We moved on to other topics. But throughout this exchange I had been struck by the fact that neither Andrea nor Vince looked at each other or raised her or his voice.

From the tone of the conversation, I felt that Andrea and Vince had had this discussion many times before, always in the same neutral tones. Vince never stood up to his supervisor and asked for a raise. And Andrea struggled along, trying to run the household with a weekly paycheck that was never enough.

Clearly, there was anger in the room, though Andrea and Vince denied it. In their own ways, however, all the children showed that they were aware of the anger. Ronnie listened eagerly whenever the parents talked about themselves or about each other. (As soon as they talked about him and how he was misbehaving, he looked bored and fidgety.) The two daughters looked very frightened. I knew they were "barometers"; whenever they were frightened, we were getting closer to the anger in the family.

Later on in therapy, we talked directly about that anger.

"Don't your mother and father get angry at you sometimes?" I asked Ronnie.

"Nope." He shook his head. "They just tell me I shouldn't do stuff."

"Well, don't they get mad at each other?"

"We don't have fights in our house," Andrea put in firmly.

I looked at Vince, who nodded. "That's right."

"Well, okay, but what about when the kids *aren't* around? Don't you fight then?"

"No," said Vince. "We don't have fights. We don't believe in them."

Again, Andrea agreed.

So here was a family that never acknowledged being angry, and a boy with some of his anger clearly out of control. Everyone in the family had been trained: they all knew there was something frightening about anger.

As the sessions went on, we learned how much Vince felt that his supervisor and everyone else at work was taking advantage of him. He felt victimized. And Andrea was secretly angry at her husband for not standing up to his boss, and, of course, she was also angry at the boss. But she never acknowledged being angry. Instead, she was "disappointed," and sometimes she felt helpless. Vince always wanted to earn more money to relieve the financial stress in the family. But he couldn't stand up for himself at work and ask for a raise. So *he* remained "disappointed"— which really translates into resentfully angry.

As Ronnie listened to both his parents, he looked terribly frustrated and squirmed in his seat.

I asked him what was the matter.

"If that was me," he said, referring to his father, "I would've punched my boss in the mouth."

It seemed pretty clear that Ronnie was using his anger to tell his father something.

As Vince worked in therapy, he began to feel better about himself—more confident of his value on the job and his value in the family. And he was finally able to get in touch with his anger, which was formidable. Eventually, Vince and his supervisor "had some words" (as Vince put it), even some angry words. Things didn't miraculously improve at work, but Vince was pleasantly surprised that he was neither reprimanded nor fired for disagreeing with his boss.

Toward the end of our sessions together, the girls became less frightened. And Ronnie became more attentive as his parents talked about their fears, about their feeling of being inadequate, and about their rage. He discovered that someone other than he was losing control in the family.

I asked Ronnie, "Have you figured out the question I asked you before? Do you know why it's fun to hit other kids?"

He squirmed in his seat and said sullenly, "I think because I'm angry all the time."

"Well, you know what," his father said loudly, "it may be fun for you, but other kids are getting hurt. And it makes me angry. I'm not going to tolerate that kind of behavior from one of my children anymore. You'll have to find something else to do with your anger."

Ronnie gaped at his father, then glanced at his mother and me. None of us said anything. He shrank back in his chair and folded his arms.

A couple of months later, the school counselor called to say that Ronnie was expressing far less anger at school. At first Ronnie had seemed very withdrawn and anxious. No doubt he was trying to find a new way to be, other than angry; he was trying to find a new identity. Later, he reached a stage where he didn't bully other kids the way he used to. His anger was a more integrated part of him. He would push back when other kids pushed him, but he had no need to prove that he was stronger than they. And then he became increasingly involved in sports, where he had an outlet for his competitiveness.

Now, it seemed, his parents were expressing their own anger, and Ronnie didn't have to be responsible for all the anger in the household.

Peter Goodman, formerly a social worker in the Mental Health Sciences Department at Hahnemann University Hospital, joined me on a show in which we talked about children's anger, especially the kind of anger that is expressed toward parents. At Hahnemann, Peter would see children like Ronnie every day, although often his patients were older and their behavior was more extreme.

"Anger in kids can cover frustration, irritation, or disappointment," Peter observed. "Often, parents are not aware how they are *replaying* their own yearnings in their children when they become parents." He went on to say that he often found himself dealing with angry kids "who really do have gaps in what's called their superego development. They don't have the 'rudimentary conscience' that causes someone to feel guilty or ashamed."

"You're seeing angry kids without consciences," I responded, "and I'm seeing adults who have a lot of difficulty with anger. I wonder whether there's a relationship between the two."

"Often it's kind of all-or-nothing among parents," said Peter. "They think they're being extremely patient because they don't see themselves as expressing anger. But unfortunately, what many parents do is turn off to their own cues. If they could let out a small amount, almost on a daily basis, they could 'let the steam out,' so to speak. Instead, the anger often accumulates until there's a tremendous explosion."

What affects the kids is their parents' inability to tolerate their own emotions. The lives of children depend on their ability to pick up what goes on inside their parents. So when their parents feel anger but withhold it, the kids walk around on eggshells. They have to figure out how to tread very, very carefully, or they'll crush the eggshells and be crushed themselves.

Among adult children of alcoholics, this "walking-on-eggshells" pattern is most visible. They feel they know *exactly* what's going on inside their parents at all times. And all those things inside the parent that aren't expressed become lies. Reality is distorted.

If children know we're angry and if we say that we're not, that's confusing to them. It's a crazy message. It's a variation on the message given by an angry parent who beats a child and says, "I'm doing this for your own good." There's just no way the child can integrate a message like that.

When my daughter Ali was about twelve years old, she went through an "I-hate-everyone" phase. She hated her teachers, her friends, the nurse, even the handyman who came to our house.

Finally I blew up at her and said, "Ali, I *hate* your hatred."

Immediately, I wondered, Why couldn't I tolerate the way she hated everything? What was I really saying? After all, it was *only* a phase, and she wasn't hurting anybody.

I needed to explore what my intolerance was really about. Why did *her* hating everything and everybody push a button inside *me?* I recalled that when I was growing up, it was difficult to have my anger acknowledged in my family. I was small physically. I was the youngest. At times I was filled with anger. It was uncomfortable for me. And I guess my anger still makes me uncomfortable, to a certain extent. So when Ali came home hating everybody, it pushed a button in me. But I was able to look inside and see what I couldn't tolerate.

I invited Ali out to lunch with me so we could talk about it. We went to Pizza Hut.

At lunch, I started talking to her about her hatred, and she denied it. She said, "It's not me. It's everybody else." Then I started to talk about what goes on with me and how troubling it is for me. I talked about some of my fears.

"Daddy," she interrupted, "when I talk about 'hating,' I don't *really* hate. I'm just a kid. I hate like kids hate. I don't hate like adults."

That was what I needed to hear. It was enough to allay my anxiety—and that was easily worth the heartburn I get from pizza.

I don't know what Ali got out of that lunch, but one thing I got was a better understanding of her rage and more tolerance for my own. I spent some time during the next four days thinking about me and my rage, rather than her and her rage. And that gave me a better understanding of the difference between hers and mine. Of course, I have no choice about my rage: I have no control over how I feel. And I can't exorcise it. But I can control what I do with my anger. And I was better able to control it when I understood the difference between my hate and Ali's hate. Each of us had his own—and if I couldn't tolerate mine, I needed to get help rather than trying to control hers.

One of the people my daughter hated, at this stage, was her own sister. They fought frequently, and, of course, there were times when I wanted to jump in, play the role of judge, sort things out, and teach them lessons about getting along with each other. I think that's a normal parental reaction, if only to dampen the racket made by two kids fighting.

But I think that when siblings fight with each other it's often something they need to do—and something that we as parents need to respect. They're carving out their turf. They're learning *how* to fight. They're learning about give-and-take in relationships.

My own sister, born five years before me, was the queen of the family when I was born, and she resented me terribly for coming into her life and taking some of the limelight off her. She loved me—and she beat me up. When I got old enough to realize she was the queen, she and I often battled. I was jealous of her. I was jealous of her achievement. We had physical fights—and we loved each other very much.

We learned aggression from one another. We learned competitiveness from one another. Through our fighting we learned how to hate each other and how to love each other. Had our parents interfered with these battles, I think we both would have been deprived of this education. We trusted each other, knew each other better than many other people do, and the loss I felt at her death continues to be one of my greatest sorrows.

I think this happens with all siblings. There is more intimacy in many sibling relationships than there is in any other relationship. These are relationships that have to be nurtured and allowed to be.

Within limits, parents need to stay out of these sibling battles. If we get too involved in sibling fighting, then it becomes a three-person fight, and therefore it never gets settled equitably. Either both children gang up on the parent or it's the parent and *one* child against the *other* child.

But what if the fighting is *not* within the children's limits? What if somebody is getting hurt?

Of course, if children go to extremes, parents need to intervene. If they're harming each other or destroying significant property (more significant than ripping up papers, and so on), then something has to be done. One child has to be protected. But this is intervention because they need you, not because you can't tolerate your own anxiety.

Not long ago, I was at a house where two sisters, seven and four, were playing with a toy stove. The older sister, Jessica, was "playing the mother," and Abbie, the four-year-old, was "playing the daughter." Everything was going fine until Jessica's friend Hayes arrived. The three girls were going to play together, but now they all needed to settle on new roles. Within a few minutes of Hayes's arrival, Abbie bit her sister and knocked over the stove. She didn't want to play with anyone—and she didn't want anyone to play with her! It turned out that Jessica and Hayes had told Abbie she now had to "be the baby" because she was the youngest. And Abbie insisted that no one would play unless she could be the mother.

When the biting started, her father stepped in. He told the older girls to leave the room while he talked to Abbie. Then he stood beside Abbie while she talked to Jessica and her friend. He didn't intervene—just empowered her by his presence. In the end, Abbie chose to play the baby. But now it was her choice, not something the older girls had forced her to accept.

Often, when a conflict reaches the level where someone is going to be hurt, it's because one sibling is unempowered. What might help a great deal is finding a way to empower that child. It could be just a wink to let him know we're there if he needs us. Or maybe we need to let him take out his frustration on us. Once he knows that someone is listening, his expressions will usually become less extreme.

And it's important to discover what they're fighting about. Maybe it's not about turf. Perhaps they're fighting over some emotional resources in the family that may or may not be there. Their arguing could be expressing some tension in that family that the parents haven't expressed up to now.

When children are most angry is when they most need someone to hear them. Whether they're angry at each other, at their parents, or at their world, *that's* when they're most eager to have an ear. And it's usually the time when we're *least* likely to hear.

If our own anger is acceptable to us, we'll be able to hear them and hear what they're trying to express. Are they trying to tell us about their frustration? Are they in a situation that's too difficult or too unreasonable? Is their anger really expressing fear—fear of failure, fear of being overwhelmed, fear of shame and embarrassment?

For us to understand what our children are expressing, we have to get past our own screens. In Ronnie's family, everyone was screening out anger to the point where they couldn't even recognize it in their son; all they saw was misbehavior. In my experience with Ali, it was another kind of screen—the adult hatred that I was carrying around prevented me from hearing about *her* kid hatred toward things, or finding out why things weren't going well for her. So these are the screens we have to get past; we have to learn how to understand and tolerate our own anger before we can begin to tolerate anger in our children. It is only when we can *tolerate* the anger that we can explore it, understand it, and provide a safe place in which our children can accept it.

24

Secrets Between Parent and Child

∾

What's secret—what's private? How much can we keep from our children and still expect them to be honest and truthful with us?

I wish I knew the answers, particularly for parents of teenagers. We know that our teenage children live in very difficult times, and we would like them to be able to confide in us. But what are the boundaries? Because all of us do have boundaries to our privacy.

Boundaries give children a clear sense of who's in charge in the family. At the same time, children need to know that the people in charge are not so insecure that they have to be rigid about those boundaries. Roles can be flexible—boundaries can be permeable. Our children have to be reassured that we as parents are in charge, and they also need to know that we're secure enough to let them see our vulnerabilities, our fears, and our feelings.

When parents withhold secrets, it's not necessarily by design. I think it's part of human nature to take pieces of ourselves we can't deal with and put them on a shelf. Usually, we put on the shelf either things we're ashamed of or things that we find too painful to deal with. Those are our secrets. Sometimes our children find those things and bring them out, and sometimes they *live* them out.

I'm reminded of Keith, a patient in his mid-thirties, who'd had a very bad relationship with his father. His father was dying while Keith's wife was pregnant. And though Keith knew his father was dying, he refused to go see him. A month after his father died, Keith's daughter was born.

Years later, Keith's seven-year-old daughter used to sit on the front steps and cry for no apparent reason. Keith asked her, "Why are you crying?"

She replied, "I miss my grandfather."

The grandfather she'd never known, never seen, never heard about. Yet, somehow, she'd reached up on her father's shelf and "found" the vulnerable part of him that had never said good-bye to his father—the grandfather she now missed so terribly.

How *do* they do it?

My daughter Debbie was going into the hospital for a tonsillectomy, and I was trying as hard as I could to hide my anxiety. As we waited around in the hospital hallway before surgery, I started pacing. She asked me, "Are you nervous about my operation?"

Being the honest family therapist who knows he can't fool his child, I said to her, "Yes, Debbie, I'm nervous."

"What are you nervous *about*?"

"Well, a number of things. I'm nervous that they might hurt you. Or you might still have colds when this operation is over. And I'm nervous you might be mad at Mommy and me."

And then she looked up at me with her big brown eyes and said, "No, you're not, Daddy. That's not what you're nervous about." And I, expecting the cutest little answer, said, "Okay, what do *you* think I'm so nervous about, sweetie?"

She said, "You're afraid I'm going to die in there. Aren't you?"

Yes, that fear was on the shelf for me. And it was up there for a reason—the idea was *intolerable*. I couldn't bear that thought. I wouldn't allow myself to think it.

So she thought it for me, and she confronted me with it. And I think that's what kids do for us over and over again. After all, their lives depend on knowing and understanding and reacting to what goes on inside us.

What if Debbie had not said that to me? She would have taken that fear of mine off *my* shelf, and she would have had it inside her when she went into the operating room. So she would have carried my fear that she was going to die. And that wouldn't have been fair!

Of course, there are times when we don't know that we're "thinking the unthinkable"—when our own feelings are just too intolerable. Often our children find ways of asking us about those feelings or letting us know that they realize something's going on with us. We're more honest with our children and ourselves when we help them explore the feelings with us, rather than trying to cut off parts of ourselves.

If I had denied being nervous when Debbie asked me, then she would have been stuck with a lie from her father. But she gave me a gift. She detected my nervousness; she asked me about it; and together we found what was on my shelf. When we did, she didn't have to carry my fear by herself; we could share it .

—◊—

Perhaps there's a way to spot what kids are going to find on the shelf before they find it—a way to recognize the secrets that feel almost intolerable to us.

The test might be to ask, What am I ashamed of? What parts of me or my life am I ashamed of? What's going on that's so painful that I haven't wanted to deal with it up to now?

Often, though, we never really deal with an issue of this kind. Instead, afraid of being judged, we wall ourselves off from the world. And as part of that walling-off process, we're not able to have contact with each other. We're keeping a piece of ourselves out of the relationship.

The only way I know to help you get through the shame is to understand—at least in your head—that whatever you're going through, many other people in the world have also gone through. Talking about what you feel shameful about is a way to free yourself from that shame.

How much more helpful it would be for Keith, whose daughter sits on the steps crying for her grandfather, if he could tell his daughter—or at least acknowledge to himself—that he had a difficult relationship with his father. Of course, if he tells his daughter, it will have to be in the language of a seven-year-old. But I think he could say to her that he still feels angry, that he still feels hurt—that he regrets, perhaps, not going to see his father when he was dying. If Keith could take that off the shelf, then his daughter wouldn't have to carry it.

Talking about shame and pain is both risky and courageous, but it truly is a ticket to freedom. Ideally, members of a family will feel safe enough and will trust each other enough to talk about what they're ashamed of.

When we talk about our shame with people in our family, it makes us more vulnerable and it also makes us safer to love. It's much easier to love someone who's vulnerable than someone who's defended, pretending to be perfect.

Being vulnerable also makes it easier to listen. That's what intimacy is all about—being able to talk and feeling truly heard. It's understanding the corners of somebody's insides that you were never able to understand before. It's seeing each other as genuine human beings rather than as images we create. And if we can allow ourselves to be more vulnerable with others in our own family, maybe it will be okay for us to trust ourselves with "outsiders," too.

What secrets are our children keeping from *us?*

This question becomes especially fear-provoking to parents of teenagers. Dr. Dina Solomon, formerly clinical director of Hahnemann Hospital's inpatient child psychiatry unit, noted that depression in teenagers is often manifested indirectly.

"In an adult," she said, "you usually see depression as lethargy—there's no energy, and people feel kind of sad and withdrawn. You *may* see that in adolescents. But very often what you'll see instead are anger and increased activity. Kids have explosions of rage; they start 'acting out' in school; and it doesn't seem to the parents as if they're depressed."

Of course, a lot of what she was describing was fairly typical of early adolescent behavior. So how do parents discriminate? How do we know when our children are depressed, or with-drawn, or just being kids?

I would hope that we can *raise children who can help us hear.* If our children are taught, for example, that whatever they say to us—or think and feel inside—is acceptable both in the family and in the world, then we'll be better able to hear them. They won't have to hide their sadness or hopelessness from us or from anyone else.

In early adolescence there are times when many children become so overwhelmed that death seems an acceptable alternative. Part of what's so overwhelming is the behavior of their peers. In addition to the clannishness and rivalry that have always plagued teenagers, they now have the ominous thrill, danger, and escape of drugs. Ali, at one point during her high school years, said to me, "Dad, you don't understand. There are just two groups—the druggies and the nerds." Whether or not these were really her only two choices, that's how she perceived the groups. For many of today's adolescents, the issues are a bit more complicated. Certainly there are the druggies and the nerds, but there now is a very large group of children who are high achievers and take drugs both to help them achieve and to help them "party" on weekends.

Looking ahead to adulthood, adolescents may feel more overwhelmed rather than less. "What's so great about being an adult?" they ask. I hear them say, "I'm growing into an environment that's killing me. I'm at high risk for cancer and I'm at high risk for getting killed."

To a teenager who's somewhat depressed anyway, there's nothing to look forward to. The pressure they're experiencing is formidable, and adulthood doesn't look great. They're under pressure now, and there's no light at the end of the tunnel.

The task for adults? I think we have to convince them that there are some good things to anticipate about being an adult. And we have to convince them through our actions, not our worry.

—⁓—

In Ali's freshman year at high school, she told me that half her friends were using drugs, and she acknowledged that these were frightening times for her.

I said to her, "Ali, these are frightening times for me, too. You're very young, but I know you'll be going to parties where there are drugs. You'll have the opportunity to use them. And I know the kids who drive will be drinking and using drugs. I can't control any of that, and it's very frightening to me."

Ali tried to allay my anxiety. "Dad, I'm scared, too. But you raised me real well and you'll just have to trust me now."

Is it okay to put a child in the position of allaying her parents' anxiety? I think it is, as long as she or he doesn't have to do it on a regular basis. If a parent is chronically anxious, vulnerable, and insecure, I wouldn't want to see the child "raise" that parent (as they sometimes do). But I wasn't asking Ali to take care of me. I just wanted to acknowledge to her and to myself that in fact I was out of control when it came to her behavior, and I didn't much like it.

We as parents often communicate our vulnerability, but we do it indirectly. If we can do it directly, and if we have children who can help us hear, then there are times when they can address our vulnerability without taking responsibility for it. We don't have to hide it from them, or keep it secret. And in return, they may feel safe in confiding their vulnerabilities to us.

25

Do Our Children Feel Safe with Us?

∾

My caller, who identified herself as Amy, said she was thirteen years old. Her parents were divorced, and she was living with her mother. She used the word workaholic to describe her mother.

"I'm not sure my mother feels good about herself," said Amy. "She always seems overworked and mad about something—but I don't know what it is. And lately she's been crying—not a lot, but, like, when we get into fights, she starts to cry really easily. I think she's feeling down. And if she started seeing a man, I don't think she'd think about me anymore. As long as she had somebody loving her, she wouldn't need me."

"Do you think you could tell your mother some of your fears about *you?*" I asked Amy. "Could you tell her some of your fears about the man she might bring in—and some of your concerns about her?"

"Well, I have," she said, "but Mom sort of doesn't really admit how she feels. I mean, maybe she can't tell me the truth. Or maybe she doesn't want to admit that she's unhappy with just her and me. It seems like she really doesn't want to tell me how she feels."

We discussed the possibility of talking to someone outside the family who might help Amy's mother with her feelings about herself.

"I'd hate to see you feel responsible for taking care of your mother and making her feel good," I said.

"Yeah, well, that's what I feel like I have to do, because she's so down lately. I feel like I'm her mother and she's the kid."

"I'd love to see it the opposite way," I said. "I think it's important for you to work as hard as you can to be thirteen—to do what thirteen-year-olds do, to act like a kid."

I told Amy that I had girls who were roughly her age. "And the best thing they do when I'm down and feeling bad is just act like kids. And I think it's terrific when they do that."

"Okay," said Amy, "I'll try."

But as she got off the phone, I wished Amy's mother had been able to hear her daughter's words. I think she would have been surprised, and I'm sure she would have been touched. And I also wondered whether Amy's mother *could* hear her daughter. Her mother's needs were so great that the girl felt that she had to become the parent. When the world feels like that, it's very unsafe for a child.

The withholding of truth is a threat to a child. Earlier, I described the craziness that children experience when their parents deny what they're thinking or feeling. I think a child can tolerate the temporary unavailability of a parent. But to hear a lie from a parent is a truly frightening experience.

Of course, the continuum runs from omissions to outright lies. At one end of that continuum is Amy's mother, who simply can't admit how she feels. At the other end is the parent who intentionally lies to conceal the truth from her child.

What comes to mind is a session with a single mother who came in with her twelve-year-old son and eight-year-old daughter. The mother described how close they all were. She praised the honesty and helpfulness of her son and daughter. Later in the same session, when she was talking about continuing therapy, the mother wondered out loud whether she could afford the fees.

Right away, the boy said, "Mom, are you frightened about money?"

"Oh, no, not at all," she answered quickly. "That's not for you to worry about. We're fine."

The boy stopped asking questions; her answer clearly raised his anxiety level. The message was, There's a problem/there's not a problem. They were a close family in the mother's view, but in order to stay close, she had to withhold anxiety from her children.

That's the kind of lie that makes a child feel crazy, guilty, and frightened. He's likely to wonder, How much money do we have? How much *don't* we have? And he'll have no guidance in dealing with the anxiety those questions raise.

We don't want to hurt our children, of course. But I think we shouldn't lie to a child about the way we experience the world, because that's what the child picks up on. When we're talking about our experience of the world, an omission and a lie are the same thing. If we feel pain or we feel overwhelmed and disappointed in our lives, then we need to tell our children, because they're going to be aware of it. And it becomes our responsibility to change the way we see the world and not lie to ourselves about it.

Of course, our children can know about us in a way that's safe to them, without knowing every detail. If we're worried about temporary financial troubles, we can tell them about our worry without involving them in the monthly budget. Children can know that Mom and Dad are having problems in their relationship without knowing that Mom has inhibited sexual desire or that Dad has premature ejaculation. If they know Mom and Dad are having trouble loving each other, they know it's something that belongs to Mom and Dad—not something they can fix or something they might be blamed for.

A colleague of mine treated a six-year-old boy who was suicidal. When the psychiatrist asked Randy why he wanted to die, he said, "I'm too much of a problem for my mom. I'm more than she can handle. Life would be a lot easier if I wasn't here anymore."

The mother had never said this to her child. She had never told him that she didn't like him or didn't want him around. Yet these were the messages that he had picked up from her unavailability. Luckily, during therapy the mother was able to say to Randy, "Yes, in some ways life would be a little simpler if I didn't have a child. But I value you. I love you. You are such an important part of my life!"

It might have been painful for Randy to hear that he made his mother's life more difficult at times, but that was important for him to know; much of his anxiety grew out of his feeling that he was making life more difficult. And it was essential for him to know how much she loved him and what an important part of her life he was.

With that conversation as a beginning, Randy and his mother began working together to explore ways in which they did enjoy each other—ways in which life was not a burden, but a pleasure. In addition, his mother finally made a commitment to begin working on her own depression, which she had been trying to keep from Randy and herself.

We may be aware of some of those times when we are unavailable to our children, but it's often hard to know *what* they find frightening. Ideally, if they are at an age when they can talk about their fears, we can ask whether they feel good about us as their parents and good about themselves. And when they feel unsafe, they may be able to ask us or talk to us about what frightens them.

And it's our responsibility to draw the boundaries in our relationship—to decide *how* we confide in our children. If we as parents confide secrets to our children and don't take responsibility for our problems, then we give our children an irrational sense of power. If a mother complains to a child about her husband—but doesn't talk to her husband or deal with the issue herself—she makes the child feel he or she is responsible.

If, on the other hand, the mother says, "Daddy's getting on my nerves. He and I are having problems, but we've talked about what's bothering us, and we're trying to work things out," it may be frightening to the child but at least the child knows that the parent is going to work on it. The child knows that the parent ultimately *is* the parent.

Claudine, a twenty-six-year-old patient, told me about her mother, who had been in a very bad marriage and had confided in Claudine all through her childhood. Beth, the mother, used to complain aloud about her marriage: among other things, she told her daughter that Claudine's father was a very poor lover, and she told Claudine that she was having an affair. She cautioned her daughter not to tell her father.

The earliest of these conversations took place when Claudine was eight or nine years old. The confidences were far too much. Claudine was being treated as an adult when she wasn't yet ready. Her mother had given her more power than any child should have. Later, as an adult trying to form adult relationships, Claudine was still dealing with her mother's issues as well as her own. When I saw her, she had been divorced once and admitted that she had a tremendous amount of difficulty in relationships. Claudine didn't feel good about herself, and she felt very protective of her mother. She had grown up being her mother's only friend.

How do we draw boundaries—and yet *not* hide ourselves from our children? Will their world still be safe if we show our weaknesses? How do we know when children feel unsafe—and how can we make the world safer for them?

If we are concerned, we can always ask them: "Do you have questions about what's happening in the family? Is there anything you'd like to know? Is there something that frightens you?" Often, they can tell us, if we are able to listen to their hearts.

I think honesty and love help to create the safety that children need just to be children. If we want them to "fix" us, to cure us, to make us better, then we are not being honest with ourselves; we know that children can't heal us or heal our relationships with others. That is beyond their capabilities, and it is certainly not their responsibility.

On the other hand, we are not being honest or loving if we hide our fears and ask them to pretend the world is different from what they see. The child of an alcoholic father, for instance, can see that the father's drinking is out of control. If the mother says, "Your father doesn't have a problem. He's just had a bad day at the office," then the child feels terribly unsafe.

But picture a mother who could say, "Your father has an illness called alcoholism, and it's out of control right now. I can understand that it's frightening to you, and sometimes it's frightening to me. I'm doing the best I can—we're *all* doing the best we can to make it better for all of us."

Just hearing that, the child feels safer in an unsafe environment.

And that's my point about honesty. I think we owe honesty to our children, because when we try to force safety on them *without* being honest, it begins to feel unsafe. When we try to hide our fears, our depressions, or our vulnerability, our children pick them up and try to take care of us.

I think we owe it to our children to be strong enough to show our weakness. If we can show that we have the kind of strength inside that it takes to talk about our weakness and our fears, then they'll feel safe in that strength. And our fears will not threaten them.

26

Children's Sexuality—What It Means to Us

~

Perhaps the most appropriate way to approach the topic of sexuality is by taking off all our clothes, then looking in the mirror.

How do we feel about *our own* bodies? Do we feel pride? Do we enjoy our bodies? Do we feel shame and embarrassment?

And if we look at our partner's body, how do we answer those questions?

And what about the sexual feelings between us? Is sex pleasurable? Is it shameful? Is it just for procreation?

This is more than an exercise in self-awareness: it's a way of beginning to understand the messages about sex that children get from us, and it's a way of understanding what their sexuality is likely to mean to us as their parents. Before we talk with them about sex, before we introduce words, we need to understand how we feel about our own sexuality.

A couple with a four-year-old son and a six-year-old daughter asked me, "How should we tell them about sex? When is the appropriate time?" They wondered whether Dad should talk to

Jimmy and Mom should talk to Molly—the "traditional" approach.

Both parents had learned about sex long before *their* parents told them anything. The mother had overheard her parents' making love when she was about the age of her daughter; within a few years she had learned all the details. The father had also learned from his young friends, and he got graphic evidence from magazines smuggled into the neighborhood. Both parents could recall the halting, inadequate "birds-and-bees" lectures they had heard from their parents about the time they reached puberty. By then, they knew just about as much regarding the physical details as their parents could tell them.

This couple felt good about the sexual relationship they now had with each other, and they wanted to be more open than their parents had been. What could they do differently?

"Well," I suggested, "why don't you *both* talk to your children? And while you're at it, why don't you hold hands?"

In order to communicate about sexuality to our children, I believe we have to share as well as teach. Children learn from what we say, from what we do, and from who we are. So if we're able to talk about it, they won't have to wonder about what goes on with us.

What messages did we receive from *our* parents?

Can you estimate how many times they made love every week? Did they make love at all? How much affection was there in the house? How did both your parents dress? Did they kiss? Did they touch each other? Was you mother a visibly sexual person? What about your father?

All those things are communicated to a young child. The child finds out whether sexuality is good or bad, pleasurable or not. The behavior of parents helps children resolve their conflicts about sexuality and to an extent determines the pleasure of first genital experiences.

As for "when it's appropriate" to talk about sexuality, I would say that it's *never* too early. One of my daughters became curious about sex when she was just a few years old. When she asked me about it, I told her everything she wanted to know in language that I thought she would understand. About a year later she asked almost exactly the same questions all over again. This went on for several years.

She couldn't accept or absorb it all the first time. She started off being confused, then being repelled, then titillated—and finally she was matter-of-fact about sex. Each of these stages of reaction was perfectly natural, given her age. And gradually, at her own rate, she was able to take it all in.

I think that with sex, as with many other things, human beings take in what they *can* take in. Children who are learning about sexuality may go through the stages that my daughter went through, from confusion to matter-of-factness. There isn't any "right time" for the right words with them. They are learning about sexuality from the moment they're born, and when they ask questions, they deserve to have their questions answered honestly.

Are there any questions about sexuality that we *shouldn't* answer? The definitive answer is, *It all depends.*

What comes to mind, for example, is the day my daughters asked me about "bopping the baloney."

It all started when Sandy and I previewed an R-rated movie, *Vacation*. We wanted to check it out before letting our daughters (then eleven and twelve) watch it on the VCR. Sandy was only troubled by a single scene in which one of the boys in the movie alludes to masturbation as "bopping the baloney."

"I don't think the girls should hear that," she said.

"Well, that doesn't bother me," I maintained. "And besides, it goes by so fast, they won't understand it." We discussed it further, but the upshot was that we allowed the girls to watch the movie.

About a week later, we were on our way home from Sesame Place (a recreational park for children created by the producers of *Sesame Street*) when a voice called from the back of the van; "Daddy, what's 'bopping the baloney'?"

With a good deal of anxiety and perspiration, I explained about masturbation—and breathed a sigh of relief when I was done. I heard some low-volume conversation between the girls. Then, a couple of minutes later, one of them sang out:

"Daddy, did *you* ever bop the baloney?"

Again, the anxiety, and after a deep breath: "Yes, I bopped the baloney when I was a kid."

Thirty seconds went by. "Daddy," a voice piped up again, "do you *still* bop the baloney?"

And at that point I decided it was boundary time: "That's my business, and not your business."

In retrospect, I feel that I probably should have been more honest with them. But at the time, I decided it was a boundary issue. And that's the point: There are boundaries to my privacy, just as there are boundaries to theirs. I think I can talk about sex without shame—at least I hope I can. But when I get to something that's just my business, I'm going to say so. And I hope they'll always feel free to do likewise.

Of course, when children begin to experience the changes that come with puberty, many of their discoveries are going to be personal and private. During those early teen years, how they deal with sexuality *is* their business. Yet, by then, they have already learned from what we do and who we are.

Roger, a twenty-six-year-old patient, grew up in a family where his parents were comfortable with their sexuality. Although the family was religious and their church was dogmatic about certain kinds of sexual behavior, the parents respected other views. They made it clear to their children that they could make choices for themselves about their behavior as well as their beliefs.

Roger's therapy was unrelated to sexual issues. During one session, however, he talked about what happened when he started masturbating, at age thirteen. He recalled feeling terribly guilty and ashamed. Masturbating felt *too good!* Surely God would strike him dead immediately! Unable to bear the suspense and anxiety, Roger began private negotiations with God. "God," he said, "if I'm doing something wrong, could you please give me a sign somehow."

He decided to ask for something specific and thought of the hill behind his house. "God," he continued, "if what I'm doing is wrong, please move that hill a few feet, and then I'll know."

During the next few weeks, Roger dutifully went out every day and measured the position of the hill. And he finally concluded that God must not have much of a problem with his masturbating, because that hill never moved.

The conflict was resolved.

Yet I wondered how much more difficult it would have been for Roger if his parents had forced him to accept the dogmatic view that masturbation was wrong. What if they had insisted that Roger subscribe to a belief system that required abstinence or punishment? His experience with sexuality would have begun with an agonizing and irresolvable conflict.

What happens when no negotiating is permissible? Often sex becomes shameful. Children may have to repress many of their sexual feelings, or they may decide to become less aware of their own sexuality. They find it difficult to resolve conflicts.

We're sexual beings from the time we're born. When a male infant discovers his penis and has an erection, the expression on his face tells us how curious he finds this and how good it feels. A girl shows the same delight when she touches her clitoris. By age three or four, children are actively exploring, trying to find out what their differences are.

When does sex become shameful? Often the messages are indirect, but clear to the child. Not long ago, a two-year-old child was visiting my house with a number of family members. The child was playing around in the bathroom, and at one point she ran naked out into the hall. Her uncle said, "Look at you! Go back in there and put some clothes on!" Even at the age of two we can get the message that there's something wrong with our naked bodies. And that tells us there's something wrong with our sexuality.

If we as parents are not comfortable with our own sexuality, we are likely to communicate that uneasiness to our children. For instance, fathers often have a difficult time dealing with their daughters' sexuality when the girls turn twelve or thirteen. It's tough for a father to acknowledge that his daughter is sexually attractive. Often fathers distance themselves and don't acknowledge their daughters. A colleague of mine, Brenda Barry, PhD, calls this "counterincest"—just the opposite of incest. Time and again in my office I hear women who say they felt very close to their fathers until they reached their early teens. Then they felt terribly hurt when their fathers drew away.

Counterincest is really the father's fear of his own sexuality. As sexual beings, we are attracted to nice bodies, both men's bodies and women's bodies. But it's very threatening to appreciate our own child's sexuality. (I was scared as hell to note that my daughters were developing breasts. They were becoming sexually attractive to me, their father!) While it may be painful for a father to acknowledge that he finds his daughter attractive, the choice is either to acknowledge that to ourselves or to go in the other direction and never touch them or hug them again.

And our children need to have their sexuality acknowledged. Their bodies go through phenomenal changes, and if their parents seem to ignore those changes or deny they're taking place, our children are likely to feel confused and ultimately shameful about their normal sexual growth and interests.

When Doris was almost nineteen, she went out on a date with her boyfriend. They did some heavy petting, and when Doris got home, her blouse was unbuttoned. Doris's father had been waiting up for her, and after one glance at her blouse, he flew into a rage. He called her a tramp and sent her to her room.

Twenty years later, sitting in my office, Doris suddenly grasped the top of her blouse and looked down at herself. Then she looked at me. "I thought my blouse was unbuttoned," she said sheepishly.

Her father never acknowledged that Doris had changed from a little girl into a mature woman with breasts. Leaving her blouse unbuttoned after her date was a signal to him: "See what's different? I'm a woman now!" And seeing her father in me, her therapist, she was still seeking the acknowledgment of her sexuality that she'd never gotten from him.

It is never too late to acknowledge positive feelings about sexuality in ourselves and to communicate those feelings to our children. A woman who called *Voices in the Family* and identified herself as a grandmother said that she felt she had "missed the boat entirely" when her daughter was growing up. She had never talked to her daughter about sexuality, and now that her daughter was married with children of her own, she hoped that she would be able to "have some dialogue with my grandchildren as they are growing up." But first she wanted to approach the subject with her daughter.

I asked the caller to take a minute and imagine what she would say to her daughter now, if she were right there and available to listen.

"I would love for her to get the feel of sexuality's being a big part of our lives. It's not just sex. It's how we feel and relate to other people in our lives—on all levels of physical and emotional intimacy."

"Let me interrupt," I put in. "Instead of 'our lives,' could you say 'my life?'"

"It's a little harder," she admitted after a pause.

"I know, it *is* harder. But you can see where it would be more honest, too. It brings it closer to home."

"I can see that now. I was trying to talk to her about *her* and her baby and her life."

"And if you talk to her about *you*—about her mother's life—it'll be riskier, but it will be very generous of you. You'll be giving her a gift rather than offering her guidance."

"I guess that's why the door was closed—because I was teaching her something instead of trying to tell her something about myself."

As this woman discovered in imagining the conversation with her daughter, it is harder to say "I" than "we" when talking about sexuality. But I agree with her: Children don't learn from lessons or teaching. They learn from what we honestly have to say about our feelings, and they learn from our behavior.

Is talk about sexuality ever harmful?

Only, I think, when we try to make our children *more* or *less* sexual than we are. With sexuality, as with everything else, if we're not happy with our own, it's probable that our children won't be happy with theirs.

Of course, our children get both good things and bad things from us—because we're human beings, after all, and we're not perfect parents. We hope we can be "good enough" parents, but we'll make mistakes. And when we make mistakes about sexuality, some of what we do may inhibit our children, and sometimes we may overstimulate them sexually. Every person is a sexual person and will understand his own sexuality in a different way. If we as parents understand that, then our children are less likely to carry our baggage.

Research has shown that girls who "act out" sexually have parents who are sexually repressed—an example of what happens if we try to make our children more or less sexual than we are. Ideally, these sexually repressed parents would acknowledge that they have their own anxiety about sex and sexuality. They might even acknowledge that they have made their own value judgments about whether sex is good or bad, and that their children don't have to adopt their values.

If we feel guilty about some aspect of our sexuality, I hope we can understand where that's coming from within ourselves and take responsibility for it. But just feeling guilty is not taking responsibility; that comes with understanding the true origins of our guilt. And when that happens, it makes sexuality less burdensome for our children. It might not heal the scars and might not undo the damage, but it will certainly open some doors in their lives.

27

The Impact of Divorce

∾

I wish I had no personal experience with the topic of this chapter. It would be far more comfortable for me to describe divorce as experienced by my patients, my callers, and the friends who have been through it.

But when I came to this chapter in the writing of this book, I had a decision to make. Sandy and I were already separated. I knew we would soon be divorced. I realized that I could not write honestly about the impact of divorce while, at the same time, concealing what was going on in my own life.

If you and I—you, my readers, and I, the family therapist—have developed a measure of rapport with each other up to now, then I suspect that you are experiencing one small fraction of what a child experiences at the moment when his mother and father say they are separating. It's a betrayal.

My daughters were fifteen and sixteen when my wife and I talked to them about it.

There were tears.

And then the sixteen-year-old looked at both of us with rage in her eyes and said: "Why did you promise us you were never going to divorce? Now you're doing it anyway!" What she was really saying was "I feel terribly betrayed, and I'm angry at you."

As much as I wish she did not have to experience this kind of betrayal, I'm happy she was able to verbalize it.

One thing children assume about their parents is that they will stay married forever and will take care of their children forever. So the issue of divorce brings on a sense of betrayal.

The impact of divorce on children is almost uniformly bad (unless there has been abuse in the family). It *can't* be good. We can rationalize and say it is better for children to live with divorce than it is for them to live with their parents in a bad marriage. Although that may be true, it's a matter of degree—one is bad and the other is more or less bad. But in no way is divorce *good* for the children. So the question becomes one of how can Sandy and I—and other divorced parents—make this experience least bad for our children.

Part of the difficulty is that our children are most needy at the outset of separation—just when we as adults and parents are most depleted and most vulnerable. Often, we've lost the person who has been our best friend. We may feel betrayed by our mate. We've lost what feels like part of ourselves.

And this is a time when we have to acknowledge our children's neediness. It's a time when everyone in the family needs his own support system and needs to be surrounded by loving people and events.

None of my experience as a therapist could fully prepare me for the neediness that I felt at the time of separation—or the neediness that my children expressed in their eyes, their words, and their touch. I knew it would be there. But I could not have anticipated its power. At the same time, my experience as a therapist told me that there were some things that could make this experience less bad for my children.

As a general statement, each parent needs to give the children ample access to the other parent. The more the children can see each parent, the better for them.

It's also important for both parents to understand that in all but the rarest cases, *both* are responsible for the demise of the marriage. Fifty percent of the responsibility is within, and fifty percent is without. Generally speaking, it was a marriage that died—not a mate who was "bad." If as parents we can grieve the death of the marriage and the death of the hope and dream, then we are less likely to blame our mate. And that's the best thing for our children.

In an earlier chapter I recalled the words of a woman who was still raging at the ex-husband she had divorced fifteen years previously and who had been dead for eight years. She still nursed rage that he had walked out on her, and she continued to blame him for the damage he had done to their sons' lives. And it seemed as if she would carry this anger for the rest of her life. This woman needed to grieve the death of that marriage—not only for herself but also for her children. As she raged at her ex-husband for his irresponsibility and betrayal, she was keeping hatred and rage alive in her children as well. And the children were helpless. There was nothing they could do to heal their mother's rage or their own.

A marriage that has died needs to be grieved. If we keep the marriage alive by blaming our mate for our pain or our loneliness, then our children will get involved in that blaming. If that happens, they lose one parent. Either they side with the parent who is saying that the other is bad, or else they defend the other parent and lose the loyalty of the parent who's doing the blaming.

There are no rules about what you can say about your ex to your children. Anyone who has been divorced must struggle with the pain, and, of course, we can't lie about that to our children. But our pain, our rage, our grief are entirely ours—they don't belong to our children. And if we're talking to them about an ex-spouse, we have to keep in mind that we're talking about their own mother or their own father.

The question is, How would you feel if someone criticized your mother? You'd be hurt and angry. Now go a step further: What if it were your own father criticizing your mother?

When you criticize your ex, that's what you're doing: criticizing your child's parent. And blaming is unfair to our children. They love their mother or father as much as you love yours. When you're tempted to blame your ex, try to hear the words as if they were spoken to you, as if someone were blaming your loved parent. In all likelihood, just hearing that way will help you recognize the limits with your own child.

During a radio program in which we were talking about stepfamilies, I invited Dr. Alberto Serrano, then psychiatrist in chief at Children's Hospital of Philadelphia, to talk about situations in which divorced parents were still fighting with each other. I told him how often I had seen children caught in the middle of this fighting. "What can we do to enhance cooperation and understanding between parents, so the children can grow and enjoy life?" I asked Dr. Serrano. "How can we get the kids *out* of the middle?"

"Often," he said, "parents don't understand that because *they* divorce, it doesn't mean the *children* divorce. Marriages and divorces are for grownups—those are *reversible* relationships. But the bond of a child with a parent and another parent is irreversible. It may be modified, but it's not really negotiable. And it's very difficult for a parent—especially a parent who feels he's being mistreated, abused, or neglected—to accept the fact that a child who witnessed all that would still be willing to have a good relationship with the other person."

Sarah, the mother of Jay, a six-year-old, told me about all the trouble her son was having in school. He had just entered first grade, and his teacher was reporting violent outbursts of aggression. When things didn't go his way, his anger was almost out of control.

I asked Sarah to tell me about her family. She and the boy's father, Henry, had been divorced when Jay was three years old. They had joint custody. Jay spent four days a week with his mother and three with his father. "He knows we don't love each other," said Sarah, "but we love him."

The mother wanted to know what she could do about her son's rage. She had remarried, and she said her present husband, Dean, was "wonderful with Jay."

I asked them all to come in.

Henry and Dean didn't look at each other when they came in the room, and they barely managed to say hello. Jay was a healthy-looking, wriggly six-year-old in jeans. He sat on the edge of his seat, his eyes darting around from his father to his stepfather to his mother.

"I don't like being dragged into this," Henry, the boy's father, announced early in the hour. "My son and I get along fine."

"Well, something's wrong," Sarah said quickly. "It must be, or he wouldn't be acting up in school."

"He's always fine around us," said Dean, the stepfather.

Throughout that first session the anger among all three was palpable. While Jay sat and watched, the two men quickly declared their anger toward each other. And part of their anger had to do with Jay's mother.

As soon became apparent, Sarah was not completely done with her marriage. She had never really said good-bye to her husband, nor fully said good-bye to her own anger.

"Do you have any affection for Henry?" I asked her during one session.

She thought a moment. "Yes, I think I do. But—"

I stopped her. "Before we find out what the 'but' has to do with, could I ask you something? What would happen if you *acknowledged* your affection?"

She shook her head and looked at me helplessly. "I don't know."

"The reason I ask," I said, "is that your marriage to Henry has ended. You've had a loss. And in order to acknowledge the affection, you might have to acknowledge the pain that goes with the loss." At a certain level, I guessed, Dean was picking up Sarah's unacknowledged affection for Henry, even though it was never verbalized. And Dean felt threatened by Henry. The second husband was competitive with the first; Dean felt he had to outdo Henry. And Henry had never really given up on his wife and had never stopped grieving.

Jay was living in a cauldron of unexpressed emotions. As these feelings were talked out, the boy felt better because he knew what was going on. He felt safer because there were three adults acting like adults, rather than three people denying their emotions.

And often, the healing comes in saying good-bye.

For months I had worked with Ruth, a very bright twenty-two-year-old who was having trouble with her college grades. Whether she would ever graduate was questionable. Ruth's younger sister was not doing well, either.

Ruth's parents had been divorced about ten years before, when she was twelve years old. There was a joint custody arrangement: she had lived with both parents, gotten along fairly well with both of them, but was still angry and resentful about the divorce. She felt bitter and betrayed.

She was also feeling frightened about forming new relationships. As can happen with children of divorce, Ruth was afraid that the same thing would happen to her that had happened to her parents—that she would eventually have to divorce. Her fear was all the greater because she didn't understand what had gone on in her parent's marriage, what the dynamics of it were.

After some months of therapy, I had her bring in her family, including her sister and both her parents. This was the first time they had all been gathered together in many years. The session seemed quiet, almost boring. We reviewed the history of what went on during the divorce. The four of them talked amicably and peacefully.

It seemed an unproductive session to me. At the end of it, I said what I'd been thinking throughout—that there seemed to be no "unfinished business," which is usually the cause of symptoms.

When it was almost time for all of us to part, I said, "Listen, we've only got another five or ten minutes together. It seems to me this is probably the last time the four of you will be together in this kind of context. How would you like to say good-bye?"

All four moved toward the center of the room. They embraced. They wept and said good-bye to each other. *That* was the piece of unfinished business in this marriage and this divorce—the unfinished business that all four of them were carrying. They had never wept, never grieved. They had turned from anger and bitterness to alienation to an "amicable arrangement." And they had never said good-bye. But when they did, all of them were finally able to move on.

Ruth returned to college and finished out her senior year. She failed only one course, which she was later able to make up. Her sister, she tells me, is also doing better. And both sisters have been able to talk to their parents and find out for themselves why the marriage died.

"It's clearer now," Ruth said in a later session, "and I'm less scared of it now. I don't know what kind of relationship is going to work in my own life, but at least I understand a part of what happened to my parents' marriage."

It's very difficult to give up on things we can't control. And that's what a divorce represents. It represents the ultimate loss of control, a marriage and a mate we can't control. And if we give up on the mate and the marriage, by acknowledging that loss, we can free ourselves of the anger and resentment—and that will liberate our children.

Finally, children are not affected by our grief and mourning. They are affected by our inability to grieve and mourn.

28

When Our Children Grow Up

∾

We hear a lot about the "empty nest syndrome"—the sudden emptiness, the not-quite-knowing-what-to-do-with-themselves that parents supposedly feel when their children leave home for the first time. But from what I hear personally and professionally, the empty nest is not as painful as it's cracked up to be.

The question is, What are you losing when your kid moves out? Earlier on, I described some of the different things that our children may mean to us. They may represent an achieving part of us that never lived to fruition; an aggressive part that was never fully expressed; a sexual part; or a part that we're troubled by and we don't like. Or they may represent the fantasy that we'll become a whole person.

So, when the child moves out, what are we losing? If our marriage is bad, we may be losing a best or an only friend. Does the child's leaving mean that we now have to deal with a spouse and a marriage that we've never really been comfortable with? Does the child's departure represent the loss of our hope that we'll ever gain control? Or is it simply the loss of a friend, the loss of a part of our life that we value, a loss of our own youth?

I think it's important that we take stock of our losses. And perhaps that's the task that we always face as our children are growing—to understand our losses, so we can realize what we gain. Then, ideally, we can appreciate what doors are open to us.

Molly Layton, a psychologist from Philadelphia, writes eloquently about a mother's reflections as her children are growing up and leaving home. In an article entitled "The Mother Journey" published in *The Family Therapy Networker* magazine, Molly reflects lovingly and unsparingly on the changes that occurred during her own journey through parenthood.

Molly Layton was a twenty-three-year-old graduate student preparing her oral report on the *Philosophical Investigations* of Wittgenstein when her first child, David, was born. She had a second child, Rebecca, three years later while still in graduate school.

Molly recalled an afternoon when David was three years old, shortly before Rebecca was born, when she was baby-sitting for her sister's children. Her two-year-old nephew had already inherited some of the clothing that David had worn when he was two—and on this particular day, he was dressed just as David used to be. Molly recalls what it was like suddenly to realize the loss of her two-year-old son:

> Suddenly I was torn open with grief merely watching my young nephew toddle down the hallway stalking the voices of his older cousins and siblings. He wore David's recently cast-off blue suit, one that I had made, and viewed from the back, with the sailor hat on his head, he was for me the two-year-old David come again. The sur-

prise was that I had not known that *that* person was gone until he magically reappeared.

So there is a bittersweet paradox at the heart of maternal thinking. The mother aches for her child's growth, but the growth is double-stranded with her joy and grief . . . The mother's rock-bottom interest in fostering the child's growth sets her up for the continual experience of separation.

And, I can add from my own experience of watching my daughters grow, this is no less true for fathers. What parents experience is not just a sudden loss when the child leaves home, but a continuum of loss from the day of birth to the days beyond the child's leaving. Our challenge, all along this continuum, is to look for the gain that comes from this journey through loss.

As the child whom we knew a year ago—or even a day ago—is transformed into other beings, we experience little deaths. Of course, the child is still alive and still with us, so we are always offered the chance to let go of yesterday's child and embrace the new one who takes his place. ("I struggled always with mothering by hindsight," Molly Layton writes, "barely sizing up one situation as the child metamorphosed into another.") And with each metamorphosis we have to find safety again—for them and for us:

> For both the mother and the infant, the tension between growing up and keeping safe is sometimes complementary, sometimes opposing. The toddler comes and goes, tumbling back into the lap of the comforting mother when he has stretched his fears too far. The mother fears

as well, sometimes experiencing the child's own curiosity as the enemy to a safe life.

In the meantime we parents are in the process of losing parts of our selves, of waking up each morning to find ourselves changed by our children. We may fantasize that we are not really changed, that we can go back to poring over Wittgenstein, immersing ourselves in the latest movies, being beach bums—whatever it was that we were before the child or children came into our lives. But part of what we have lost is the part of our identity that is the person-without-children. The parent we are now has a life inextricably entwined not only with our past life and our private selves but also with the lives of our children. And with that entwinement comes the metamorphosis:

Often I felt dumber than dirt. Could Rebecca spend TWO nights in a row sleeping over at friends'? "Duh, I dunno, gee, I have to think about that, duh." How could a person who wrote about Wittgenstein have a brain that just folded in on itself like that, pummeled by an eight-year-old's torturous pleas? My guts said, keep her home, but why? Isn't this just a tad over-involved? Why not give in? Indeed, why not just let her drift from house to house on the block, eating white bread, wearing dirty borrowed clothes, while I . . . I . . . get a massage! Wade in the surf, high-heeled shoes tossed on the beach! Not brave or selfish enough to head for the beach, instead, pestered and squinty-eyed, I was forced to think about our rules, think about reasons, make decisions, revise decisions, change my mind, hold fast, explain, insist, give up, clamp down.

Later, on the continuum of loss, comes adolescence—with the slamming of doors, the outbursts of anger, the moody silences. Separation is taking place, and it's usually painful for us:

> On these dreary occasions, I hated many of the feelings I had: I hated it when someone was not home when they agreed to be home, I hated worrying about accidents and city psychopaths, I hated seeing college applications languishing under piles of phonograph records, I hated the worries about drugs and alcohol.

And then comes the separation that feels most final, when they are leaving home for the first long trip, or for college, or for the job that will take them far away.

With each crisis of separation, it's time to regroup, to stop and consider what's at stake. What are the losses and what are the gains for us and our children?

When our children finally leave home, separateness is at a premium for them. It's important for them to form their own identity and find their own values—to discover that there's a world outside their parents and their parents' values. In order to achieve their separateness, they might need to give voice to anger they've never expressed; and, ideally, somewhere down the pike, they'll also be able to speak of love they never expressed.

More often than not, it's disrespectful to them—and disrespectful to their struggle with their tasks in life—if our own anxiety as parents makes us cling to our children. It's disrespectful if we demand more intimacy than they're willing or able to give. Too much involvement with our children is not an act of love—it's an act of selfishness.

I once worked with a family in which Ellen, the mother of two, was very unhappy with the marriage. She said everyone was always making demands on her, and these demands were constantly pulling her different ways. She said she did not have any of the things she wanted for herself. She continually feared the disapproval of her husband and her parents, and at the same time she looked to them for guidance in everything she did.

When we talked about how she spent her days, she referred to daily phone conversations with her mother. I asked what she and her mother found to talk about every day, and Ellen said they mostly just visited and gossiped. Her mother asked Ellen questions about her grandchildren: How were they doing in school? Did they have adequate clothing? Did they need anything? And she asked about Ellen: How was she feeling? Was everything all right at home? Was she managing all right?

These daily calls had been going on for years, always initiated by Ellen's mother. Clearly, her mother had a great deal of anxiety. She might be telling herself, her friends, or her husband that she called every day because she loved her daughter so much. But what she may have been doing was trying to manage her own sense of emptiness. Perhaps she felt she had been abandoned by her daughter, or perhaps she felt she had been abandoned by her own mother. The constant phone calls were actually more about anxiety than love. And the mother's anxiety contributed to making her daughter feel less confident, less adult, and less independent.

When our children finally do leave home, it's important to understand what that means to us and to get our own support for that. We need to be able to say good-bye in our own way. We're not going to be able to see them as often, to talk to them as frequently, or to know them as well. And that's as it should be, if they're going to grow in their own right and become whole parents to their children.

One spring day, shortly before her daughter left for college, Molly Layton was taking a walk by herself on Forbidden Drive near Wissahickon Creek when she realized with a shock that Rebecca's departure was only a month away.

I walked along Forbidden Drive thinking of all the wise and memorable things I still wanted to teach Rebecca: Travel abroad whenever you can. Learn the names of wildflowers. Watch out for the big trucks and tanks. Talk to your teachers. Did I tell her well enough how afraid I am of nuclear war? My neglect was so vast, it made my teeth ache. But I did not remember to say it all, and we were caught in time's implacable grind. Before us was a slant of light, an open door. *There was no shutting it.* Our life together was measured then in weeks. My physical grief was bound only by the thrill of watching my last child step into the glare of a vast and uneasy world.

29

Making Peace with Our Children

❧

At some point in our lives as parents, we need to become comfortable with the fact of living among strangers. Of course, we know these strangers to a certain extent and we're familiar with their ways. Still, there are many parts of them that we don't know, and ideally we will discover those parts. We will make peace with those parts and also make peace with ourselves as parents. That process is what's so exciting and so frightening about being parents.

Once you've made peace with your children, then and only then can you truly appreciate who they are and appreciate their differences. Perhaps what you can appreciate is their willingness to explore the world more than you did, or perhaps their ability to take more risks than you. Or on the other side, perhaps they're more conservative or more cautious than you. And if you're saddened by that, it doesn't mean it's wrong for them.

Having children is a terrible and exciting gamble. It's a genetic, biochemical roll of the dice. Our children grow up in worlds that are different from ours. They see the world initially through our eyes, our spouse's eyes, and their older siblings' eyes. And then they develop eyes of their own.

When they come into the world, we have wishes that they'll be everything we never were—and fears that they'll wind up like alcoholic Uncle Harry. And we assume that they'll see the world in the same way we do. But somehow they wind up making their own paths. Of course, we don't want them to get hurt as they make their way along those paths—but what can we do? What help can we offer them?

I think we owe it to our children to share our wisdom. If we share our wisdom for the purpose of changing our children, then that's hitting them over the head with a hammer or shoving something down their throats. If the wisdom turns into advice, that's selfish. But if we simply share ourselves and let our children know our hearts, then it's a gift. And I think it's a gift we're responsible for giving them.

In everything I've said about children, I've often repeated how important it is to hear their hearts. Consistent with that, it's important to see what they're doing as they start to make their own paths. That's where their hearts lie! Their paths differ from ours by definition. It's unfair to them and unfair to us to try to wrestle them back to our path.

At some point in our lives, we need not only to give up the expectation that our children will live out our fantasies but also to acknowledge the paths that they're taking. Some of our fantasies have to do with what we would like to have for ourselves, but most unacknowledged fantasies may simply be assumptions. Do we assume that they will accept our lifestyle, our views, our likes and dislikes? Do we expect them to have similar beliefs, hold a similar position in society, or to follow our example in creating a family of their own? Or perhaps we have always thought that our children would make the perfect family for themselves, and that we would feel happier and stronger when we could see them safely settled in with their own families.

For a segment of *Voices in the Family* that dealt with gay and lesbian sexuality, one of my guests was Dr. Tom Sourman, from the Philadelphia chapter of the international organization of Families of Lesbians and Gays (FLAG). I asked Tom how he had reacted when his own son, at the age of sixteen, told him that he was gay.

"My response was shock," the father said. "I remember my knees literally shook. And for the first six months or so, my thinking was very egocentric. I was much more concerned for myself than I was for him."

I asked him to look at the shock. "If somehow you could have grabbed yourself at that moment and looked at what was going on inside you, what would you say?"

"I think what I was facing was my own homophobia," said Tom. "For forty years, I had simply bought the myth that society had taught me about gay men. And now I realized that the young man living under my roof was also gay—and he was a child whom I loved very much. And that was shocking to me."

Later in that program, Tom talked about the part of the fantasy of his family and his child that he lost when his son told him he was gay. "I think I lost an illusion that all parents have for their children—I mean, that our own kids are going to grow up and be rich and famous and be brain surgeons and go to the moon and make great Nobel Peace Prize contributions and everything else. And part of that illusion is they're going to be heterosexual, and they're going to have a family, and they're going to provide us with grandchildren. There is no reason why my son can't be rich and famous and win a Nobel Peace Prize, if that's where his work and his talents take him. But the heterosexual part and the grandchildren from him won't be possible."

So part of the shock for Tom had been the death of the "ideal" family.

"I don't think any family can grow unless you go through that death of the ideal," I said on that program. "If you keep that ideal in your head and you keep trying to plug everyone into that ideal, then no one can be real."

As our children turn even five or six degrees away from us, we have to be aware of our fear and our excitement and our hope for them. And as that five or six degrees turns into ten or twenty degrees, even ninety degrees, we have to monitor those feelings every step of the way—and ultimately realize that our child is another human being and not necessarily an extension of us.

It's something that we don't have as much control over as we would like—and we never will. Once we can acknowledge that, we can appreciate these human beings much more. But again, part of listening to their hearts has to do with first being loyal to yours—understanding what's in your heart, your struggles, your guilt, your fear, your pain. And then the challenge is to be yourself with your children—not to try to hide those parts of yourself. Because the more of you that you show your children, the more vulnerable you allow yourself to be, the safer their world will be. They will be able to use their wings both to fly away and to return.

It's easiest to make peace with your children if you've made peace with every deviation in that path they're taking, every step of the way.

—⁂—

What we provide for our children, I believe, are roots and wings. Roots—to grow, to be, to come back to if they feel the need. Wings—the security of a safe place to leave when they need to and the confidence that they can fly.

And we don't want to weigh them down with our baggage. If we do, their wings aren't going to work very well.

As Molly Layton described in "The Mother Journey," each step a child takes is a loss for the parent. If we don't acknowledge that loss within us, then it becomes a loss for the child. If we don't let the child walk away from us to develop his own identity, then he's going to be stuck rebelling against ours.

In the ending phase of therapy with me, a patient gave me this poem. She said it described her experience in therapy; ideally, it would also describe the experience of any child who has found his wings:

Come to the edge—
No, we might fall.
Come to the edge—
It's too high.
Come to the edge,
And we came,
And he pushed,
And we flew.

❧

PART FOUR

Our Selves

30

Our Place in the Family, Our Place in the World

∿

*As sure as the flower is drawn to the sun, it is the
tropism of human beings to seek wholeness.*

—Franklin Abbott

Some facts of nature we take for granted.

We take it for granted that a seed tossed on the ground will
figure out what to do next. The plant that grows from that seed
will somehow "know" which way is up. Some inner growth
mechanism tells the plant to send its roots down into the earth
and its stems, leaves, and flowers up toward the light.

All this is knowing-without-knowing, of course. A seedling
understands nothing, and it doesn't need training. It grows in the
way it must. No matter which way a seed lands on the ground, it
responds to gravity and weather conditions by sending roots
down and it responds to light by sending leaves *up*.

These responses are called *tropism*.

How do we acknowledge the tropism in ourselves? What is it
within us that makes us reach for wholeness? Why do we grow

the way we do? It's not something we can practice until practice-makes-perfect. It just happens.

We do acknowledge human tropism in our language. We often feel a strong reaction when we feel we are "going against our nature." That feeling can be powerful even when we don't fully understand what "our nature" really is.

How do we orient ourselves in the world? How do we "know" what we need for our own nurture and growth? And how do we know when we are going against our nature? What is this tropism inside us?

In order to see it, we may need to make a journey inward to find our identity.

When I got out of the hospital and went back to work after my accident, I was faced each day with questions that could not be answered by looking at the person I had been previously. Before my accident, I had a role that was composed of my parents' expectations, my peers' expectations, and society's expectations. All those expectations made up the "old seed" of my identity.

When I had my accident, I was stripped of that identity. A new seed was planted, and this one was called "quadriplegic." But what was the tropism of that new seed? What kinds of "roots" and "flowers" could grow from a quadriplegic? How much could I grow—and in which direction? What could a quadriplegic do?

There was so much I needed to understand about this new self, so many questions I needed answered. How many hours is a quad supposed to work? Does a quad take naps? Is a quad entitled to cancel a lunch date because he just doesn't feel like going to lunch, or does he have to be sick? What other kinds of idiosyncratic behavior is a quad entitled to?

The only way to find answers was to *allow* the new seed to take root—not *force* it to take root. As I watched the seed begin to grow, I had to listen to it. I had to listen to my body and to my emotional needs, too. So if my body felt tired, I needed to rest. If I felt too anxious, too depressed, or perhaps just too insecure to go out to lunch, that was my body and my spirit talking. I watched and I listened, and I began to understand my new identity.

If I had tried to force the roots to grow, I would have decided what I *should* do, and then I would have tried to run my life that way. I might have told myself that I *should* work forty hours a week because someone had told me that I'd feel better about myself if I did. Or that I *should* always keep my lunch dates because I'd feel a greater sense of accomplishment. Or perhaps I would read a good book telling me "How to Be a Successful Quad" and figure out what rules I should follow. Whenever the roots are being forced, a lot of *should*-ing goes on. But when that happens, we're not listening to ourselves or allowing our roots to grow in their own way.

After a while, I started to discover what my life as a quad was going to be like. Then, just when I thought that I understood it for sure, something unanticipated would unfold.

One day, for instance, I went out to lunch with a nurse who had taken care of me when I was in the hospital. I picked her up in my van, drove both of us to a restaurant, and paid for lunch. After lunch I dropped her off at the hospital.

It was a thoroughly enjoyable lunch. I felt terrific. And on the way home, I started to cry.

I cried so hard I had to pull off the road. And I didn't understand why.

Several months later, I was thinking about it and still wondering why. And I realized that after my accident, I had assumed there would be a certain amount of constant pain in my life. I had assumed that some areas of joy would be unavailable to me, that the kind of joy I'd felt at lunch that day was not possible. These assumptions were violated, and when that happened, I was frightened and confused. When I cried, it was from confusion, fear, and other emotions, rather than from sadness.

The seed had grown more than I had thought possible. Reaching for wholeness, I had found a joy that I had thought would forever remain beyond reach. My new self had created itself, springing new roots from its own beginnings.

But why had I felt so much confusion and fear?

I had a patient who talked about the experience of "losing her old self" as if describing an old house crumbling around her. She said she felt as if she were standing in a building that had started to tremble and fall. She felt shaky and emotionally unstable. She wanted to run, but she couldn't. And when the entire building had finally fallen, she felt as if she were left standing naked.

That was what was happening to me. The building was shaken; it was crumbling around me. The confusion and fear came from the feeling that everything around me was unstable. I was left standing naked as the old self crumbled. Now I had to become the architect of my new self.

Where does our sense of self come from? And how do we know whether the identity fits us?

Initially, we learn about ourselves from the family. In a family we are expected to perform certain ways, to fulfill certain roles. There is an archaic sense of self, grown within the family, that we carry out of the family and into the world.

If our family judges us by what we do rather than who we are, the expectations may be so high that there's little room to breathe. Were you supposed to be the star performer? The healer? The peacemaker?

Or—how about the other side? Were the expectations for you very low? Were you expected to "act out" as Uncle Johnny did? Did your friends and family reinforce the idea that you were "bad"? Did your family assume that you wouldn't be competent or adequate, or that you would only perform as well as your father or mother?

Perhaps your parents expected that you would wind up as depressed as one of them had. Or maybe they expected that you would have the strength and emotional resources to pull a parent out of depression.

What are the consequences of those expectations? How do they influence your identity, your "sense of self"? Suppose I played the role of "healer" in my family—that is, if I came home from school and Mom was depressed or Dad was drunk, I could always be counted on to pull the family together and to keep things on an even keel. Or perhaps my sibling was always acting out, and everyone counted on me to be the "dependable one," the "good student." As I grew up, I would continually try to be the "good one." I would wrap this mantle around me. This might not be who I really am, but that's how I've learned to behave.

What happens then when I discover that I'm not really as good as everyone in my family expects me to be? I might feel great shame and try to hide parts of myself that feel "not good enough." That shame could turn into withdrawal, depression, insomnia, or even physical symptoms. This kind of shame can frequently have an impact on most marriages.

What's happening is that something inside me is trying to tell me that the mantle doesn't fit. I begin to discover that I'm just plain tired of being so good. Underneath that mantle of goodness are anger and resentment, which are causing my symptoms. And when I start to realize that the mantle I've been wearing doesn't fit me, that realization can be very frightening.

Marybeth was a thirty-seven-year-old patient who battled this fear in therapy. All along, Marybeth's mother had expected her daughter to become a housewife with children. The mother was a religious woman who had brought up Marybeth to be a devout Catholic and had expected her daughter to remain true to the faith.

When Marybeth started seeing me, she was a divorced professional woman who had given up all religion. Her mother was angry and disappointed, and Marybeth continually battled with her mother to gain the respect she'd never had. She was trying to change her mother into someone who would respect her and acknowledge her. She felt hurt and not understood in the context of the relationship with her mother.

Originally, Marybeth had said that what she wanted from her mother was respect and affirmation. But what she really wanted was her mother's approval for what she was doing. She wanted her mother to approve of the way she was growing, and she was furious because she didn't get that approval. Deep down, Marybeth had wanted her mother's guidance.

As Marybeth worked in therapy, we watched the roots begin to grow. She developed her own feelings about religion, which were different both from the feelings of a rebellious Marybeth and also from what she perceived as the doctrine of a rigid mother. Marybeth moved a few steps toward religion. As we watched the roots grow further, she began to understand her own values about relationships and about her career. She found her own meaning in life. The process was fraught with anxiety and ambivalence. But when the roots took, the flowers started to grow toward the sunlight.

One day Marybeth said, "Somehow my relationship with my mother is better than it ever was before. I feel like we're almost two peers or two friends—and not mother and daughter."

A change had taken place in Marybeth. She was more comfortable with who she was, and she had given up her need to change her mother.

The change in Marybeth was that she learned to respect and accept herself first, rather than continue in her struggle to change her mother. Instead of hoping for her mother's approval, Marybeth took responsibility for her own life. She made decisions on her own, and she accepted the rights and wrongs of those decisions. And when that began to happen, she could relate to her mother as adult to adult, and not just as child to mother.

In all likelihood we will never find peace with ourselves as long as we're playing the role of the archaic self. We have to give up hope of getting something we never got from our family and the hope of changing our family. Once we give up those hopes—frightening as this is—we begin to find ourselves.

To make peace with ourselves, we need the courage to run the risk of disappointing and alienating our parents and even our friends. (In fact, we rarely do alienate them, but it still takes courage to run the risk.)

Shedding the archaic self and finding the adult self is a selfish process, but not "selfish" in the sense that it happens at the expense of others. It's selfish because we're addressing the self—acknowledging the self—and the process is something that we can only do by ourselves.

In Morita therapy, which originated in Japan, a patient begins treatment by spending a large block of time alone in a room. The process of finding the new self begins there. Unlike Western therapies, which try to reduce symptoms, Morita therapy helps develop character that can be more resilient and tolerate whatever arises.

I think we all have to go away alone to find the self. I don't think there's any other way. Human beings have been doing this for thousands of years. Even in the animal kingdom, there's the moment when the immature animal must go on its own, to find its own way.

Finding the self is a lonely piece of business. It's a journey inward. In order to take that journey, we have to be courageous enough to be vulnerable. We have to trust our psyches and our spirits. We have to trust that the tropism is there, that growth will happen, that it is our spiritual, unconscious mind that will guide us on that journey.

A self doesn't appear without a struggle. We can't borrow an identity from the family archives. And it's very difficult to choose ourselves over our parents. At some point in the journey, we are likely to appear disloyal to the family. The self that emerges may not be at all what we expected to find, and that's when our family may say to us, "You're just being selfish."

When we are adults, we can address the issues of disloyalty and selfishness. We can say to our parents, "In what way am I hurting you? In what way are you feeling deprived? What can I do?" Then we can ask ourselves what we're able to do to address that hurt.

Marybeth's struggle to grow and to find her adult self was also a struggle for her mother. Her mother felt a loss, and she had to grieve her loss. When she did, Marybeth's mother was able to rejoice over what she had with her adult daughter, which was a whole new relationship.

I don't think any parent ever ends up with the child he fantasized having. There has to be some loss. In most families, however, the parent-child relationship goes through the evolutions and the losses to emerge as a whole new relationship. Eventually the parents, too, are able to give up their child's archaic self. If they truly love and appreciate the child, they will be able to acknowledge the change, respect the adult self, and rejoice in the life that their child has found.

31

What Do We Do with Anger?

∾

"Are you angry?"

When I ask that question of patients or callers, often it's when they haven't raised their voices, threatened anyone, or even sounded particularly angry. They may be talking quite calmly. Often they're simply describing the end of a relationship. Or the death of someone they loved. Or the loss of some fantasy that they acknowledge will probably remain unfulfilled.

There is usually a pause after I ask that question. Sometimes the person will honestly answer, "No, I'm not angry." Other times, he'll say, "I'm not angry, but I'm frustrated."

Frustration is a variation on anger—it's "socially acceptable" anger. So, sometimes, if we can't acknowledge that we're angry, we'll acknowledge that we're frustrated.

When I ask, "What are you frustrated about?" or "Who are you angry at?" I get many different answers.

In the case of a serious illness or the death of a loved one or the loss of a relationship, people are likely to deny that they have any right to be angry.

"I shouldn't be angry," they say. "That person didn't mean to harm me." Or "I can't be angry—it's illogical."

The caller may talk about the person he's angry at: "I can't be angry at someone who died," or "I shouldn't be angry at an alcoholic. He can't help it. He's sick."

What people are really saying is that they're afraid of their own anger. They're afraid of their impulses. They find it shameful to be angry.

Can they acknowledge how much they fear their anger? If so, then we can talk about what they fear.

All of us are angry sometimes. We may not recognize what we are angry *about;* we may not admit to ourselves that we know who or what makes us angry. Yet when asked directly, we can often see anger for what it is, acknowledge it, and sometimes even enjoy it.

Why is it often so difficult to acknowledge anger? Why, I wonder, do we feel ashamed or frightened when we feel it? Despite the fact that we feel that anger is shameful, it is a large part of our lives. Perhaps it starts when we are infants and the nipple is pulled out of our mouths. That's the first injustice we suffer, and we're angry! Everything felt okay up until then.

Most of us acknowledge that if we hold in our anger, it can lead to depression or addiction—or we may have somatic symptoms such as ulcers or colitis. And we know that if anger comes out inappropriately, we can hurt ourselves, lose our jobs, ruin our marriages, and we may hurt other people physically or emotionally. We don't want any of those things to happen.

So where do we "put" anger? What can we "do" with it?

When there's no one to rage at and no one to blame, we can probably find ways to rage at fate without doing any damage. Throwing pillows is fine. So is banging on the walls or throwing a tantrum.

But none of that cures the anger.

What we're angry at is the injustice in the world, the injustice that has affected us. And I think what we have to do is simply to feel entitled to be angry. Being angry doesn't mean we're wrong. We just have to acknowledge that our anger is there. We can't pretend that it shouldn't exist.

Injustice has happened to us, and it has made us angry. That anger becomes part of our personalities.

I consider myself an angry man. When I was a boy, I was the short kid in the playground who was always beating up kids and getting beaten up by them. By the seventh grade my nickname was "Killer."

When I broke my neck, I got even angrier. I secretly enjoyed confronting a person who had hurt me or someone I loved. If I wrote an angry letter or made an angry phone call and told that person what he'd done, I liked to think that he'd lose a night's sleep.

So many of us grew up in families where the message was "Don't worry—be happy!" . . . and above all, *"Don't be angry!"* Our schooling or our religious training may have taught us not to be angry. Society reinforces those messages.

But what happens when we can't permit ourselves to feel angry?

When we have learned that anger is unacceptable, not to be tolerated, we deprive ourselves of the full range of human emotions. But our psyches won't permit us to erase anger, and if we refuse to acknowledge and accept that emotion, it can become toxic.

I once treated a priest who had broken his neck. He was very angry, and he was overcome with the depression and guilt triggered by his anger. He felt betrayed by God, and yet he didn't feel that it was right to rage against God.

When I asked him what he prayed for, he said he prayed that God would take away his rage. He felt that he was defective for being angry and that he was betraying his vows. In his family and in school he had been taught that anger was not permissible. So he wanted to purge himself. He had to exorcise that part of him that was shameful.

In therapy I asked whether he would like to hear God differently. I wished he could have heard his God give him permission to be fully human. I wondered whether he could first be angry at God and then forgive Him—and trust that God would love him even if he was angry.

It didn't happen. He continued to be guilty and ashamed of what he was feeling, and he was consumed by his anger. He stopped therapy, because he couldn't tolerate the permission I was giving him to feel angry. Eventually it cost him his functional life. He went into a nursing home—which he didn't need to do. He was young and energetic. But his inability to tolerate and accept his anger was poisonous to his whole being.

Holly, a patient who had been an incest victim, told me, "I was very numb for many years. I didn't feel anything. And then, for some reason, at age twenty-seven, all this stuff just came bursting forth."

Holly had eating binges. For periods of time, she could control her weight. "Then something out of the norm happened. It seemed like my personality went out of control. When this anger came, I overate. I over-everythinged! No matter what I did, I overindulged in it."

I noted that one thing eating does is to help keep the feelings down—in other words, it prevents us from feeling our feelings.

"The question I have of you," I said, "is about those times when the anger is coming up and you're using food to keep it down. What would happen if you lost control of the anger? What would happen if there were no food?"

"What would happen? I think I would probably become irrational."

And we talked about her "irrationality."

I asked her what it would mean if she became irrational. She said she was afraid she would rant and rave—she'd "go crazy."

And what else?

Holly began to cry. She said she wanted to hurt her father for molesting her—she wanted to kill him. She hated the part of her that wanted to scream and rant and rave and kill. That wasn't tolerable to her.

But as she wept, Holly was able to accept her anger. She became less frightened of it.

She hadn't been overeating because she was angry. She had been overeating because she was afraid of anger. As she became less afraid in therapy, she no longer felt as if her personality was "out of control." She was able to trust herself a little more.

In the family that Holly had grown up in, anger could not be acknowledged. The incest only increased the necessity of "maintaining an appearance," especially the appearance of tranquil family happiness. No one in her family was allowed to "ruffle the waters." All of Holly's anger had to be kept inside, where it built up and felt irrational.

In all likelihood, Holly will always have to struggle with being less afraid of her anger. The most difficult thing for her was to show her anger to a friend, a loved one, or even an enemy.

Eventually she discovered that she could say, "What you just did made me angry. Please don't do it anymore."

And she discovered that when she could express her anger openly and directly, she was more comfortable with it and more tolerant of it. Anger didn't have to be a catharsis (flying into a rage, yelling, hitting), and she didn't have to "swallow it up" inside her (which led to overeating, bingeing, overindulging). When she could express her anger in a way that felt appropriate to her, she could feel comfortable with it and more comfortable with herself. Not only could she tolerate her anger, but she felt more self-respect.

It was difficult for Holly—as it is for all of us—to realize that anger can't be replaced with other, more acceptable emotions. The priest who broke his neck longed to have his anger replaced by love, to have his rage at God replaced by love of God. Holly would have liked to purge her anger, to fill herself up with other feelings that would take the place of her rage. But we can't replace anger any more than we can replace joy. If we try to replace it, we end up smiling when we feel hatred. We end up praying to God when we want to curse Him.

It's frightening to acknowledge feelings, and it's *always* frightening to acknowledge anger. But what else can we do? It's part of who we are—and we can't change who we are, or we'll lose something.

Anger is part of the passion of life. When I ask a caller or a patient, "Are you angry?" I'm asking whether he can acknowledge that passion. When we can't or don't acknowledge it, we're cutting off a piece of ourselves. If that "surgery" were successful—and I don't believe it can ever be—then it would be terribly sad, because there would be less of us to offer the world and our loved ones.

32

When We Feel Guilt

∾

Chip's mother was a depressed, chronically unhappy woman.

On Chip's twenty-fourth birthday, she bought him two neckties, one designed by Evan-Picone and one designed by Giorgio Armani. About a week later, when his mother was coming to visit, Chip decided to please her. He went to the tie rack and, after a moment, selected the Evan-Picone. He was wearing the tie when he met her at the airport. When his mother got off the plane, she took one look and sighed. "I guess you didn't like the other one," she said.

Of course, what this story makes clear is that Chip is helpless. It isn't possible for him to please this woman. His behavior can't change her feelings. He didn't do anything "wrong" to make her unhappy—and there's nothing he can do "right" that will change her mood.

Chip's mom has made her son feel guilty. But what can he *do* about it?

The psychiatrist Frank Pittman once made the observation, "There's nothing wrong with guilt, as long as it doesn't last more than five minutes and it changes your behavior."

The beauty of this statement is that it undercuts what we usually consider the ground rules of guilt. Isn't guilt, by definition, something that nags and harries us, even though we can't do much about it? Instead, Pittman tells us guilt is fine if we start to *do* something about it (in the next five minutes!). If we can't, why shouldn't we just give up our guilt?

At first glance, this sounds like a prescription for Chip. Since his guilt isn't going to change his behavior, why shouldn't he just give it up? The trouble is, his guilt probably won't vanish, even if Chip recognizes he can't do anything about it. He can't "stop" feeling guilty.

We need guilt. It's a very important creation of the superego, of the conscience. Guilt is what holds our society together. But when we suffer from guilt, most of us are suffering from too much of it. And if it's the kind of guilt we can't do anything about, wishing it away doesn't work.

Guilt is something that our psyches don't handle very well. We just aren't very efficient with it, and there's no "program" that's likely to cure it.

The story of guilt—where it resides in our being, what makes it so powerful, what makes it grow or diminish—is really the story of an age-old struggle within ourselves, our lives, our families, and even our culture.

For some time I worked with a man who was preoccupied with the guilt he felt from a childhood experience. When Andy was eight years old, he had gone swimming with his twin brother in the local swimming hole, which was forbidden. They swam out to the middle of the pond, and Andy's brother couldn't make it back. Andy tried to save him. His brother drowned.

The details of what happened during those few terrible minutes of Andy's life were replayed in his memories and his nightmares for the next forty-five years.

When Andy began seeing me, he had no hope that his guilt would diminish, much less vanish. There was nothing he could "do" that would change the past. Yet each time he replayed the scene, he would ask himself questions that implied the past could be altered: "What could I have done differently? How could I have saved my brother?"

What he wanted to change was the way he felt. He wanted the pain to diminish, so he would not always have to carry it with him.

Most Holocaust survivors have some degree of "survivors' guilt." So, too, do people who survive plane crashes, fires, earthquakes, or any cataclysmic event in which some were spared and others perished, purely as a matter of chance. Our minds search for some logic in this event: "Why was *I* the one who was spared? What makes my life worth saving? What more could I have done?" Even though they had no choice, survivors often feel as if it was "them or me": "If only *I* could have been killed—then my brother would have lived."

As Andy grew up, his memory of what he "could have done" to save his brother became increasingly distorted. He had been only eight years old when the event happened, a young boy gripped by fear and panic in a moment of emergency. But the man who recalled that moment was neither benign nor forgiving toward the boy who had experienced it. Whenever Andy projected into the past, he thought of himself as someone who was stronger, more capable, level-headed, and competent than he could possibly have been when he was a boy.

He had never said good-bye to his brother. Andy missed his twin almost continually. For the rest of his life, he had longed for a brother to confide in, to compete with, to share things with. Andy's guilt, his sense of responsibility, helped to keep this perfect companion alive.

If Andy were ever to consider giving up his guilt, he would have to give up the delusion that he had control over the events that happened when he was eight years old. And he would also have to give up his brother. He would finally have to say good-bye.

In Andy's case, guilt was a way of avoiding grieving and avoiding acknowledging his helplessness and powerlessness. His guilt was a way of not acknowledging the chaos that life can bring.

In therapy, Andy finally found a way to say good-bye to his brother. His guilt was allayed, but his anxiety wasn't—because he now acknowledged how unpredictable the world was. And in this unpredictable world, he would always be susceptible to loss. So there would always be anxiety. That was the price he had to pay for giving up his guilt.

There's so much in life that we *can't* control. How does guilt "save" us from anxiety about all that?

Some time ago, I had an accident in my wheelchair that I first blamed on myself—and felt guilty about. I had been outside, taking the dog for a walk, on a wet, drizzly day. When I came into the garage, the wheelchair tires were slippery. I accelerated the chair back and forth on the concrete to dry off the tires. The chair flipped over backward, throwing me out. I was seriously injured, and it took me weeks to recuperate.

Later, I wondered whether I was suicidal at an unconscious level. Why had I gone back and forth so quickly? Was I trying to hurt myself? A couple of analyst friends raised the same question. My father reminded me that if I'd been using a manual wheelchair (as I was "supposed to"), the accident would never have happened. So I felt terribly guilty about the pain I inflicted, not just on myself but also on my loved ones. Guilty—and also frightened by my own subconscious.

About a month after I had recovered, I was driving around in the chair when the brakes suddenly locked up. I realized then that the brakes had caused the accident. It was the result of a mechanical failure that had nothing to do with me or my unconscious.

The guilt dissipated. The accident *wasn't* my fault. But as I gave up the guilt, something else took its place. Guilt had given me the illusion of control over the world, and without that illusion, all my fears about being out of control came rushing in. I realized this kind of thing can happen to me anytime! And I was left with my sadness about how vulnerable I really am.

Implicit in Frank Pittman's advice about dealing with guilt is the reassurance that none of us is responsible for original sin. Our power and control in this life are very limited.

We have no control over our parents' pain. And if our mate is depressed, we have no control over that, either. We do not have control over our own destructive thoughts or our feelings of hostility. A lot of the issues of guilt have to do with the feeling that we have more influence than we really do. When we begin to realize that fact and to accept the undeniable truth of our helplessness, then ideally our guilt will diminish.

However, we also need to look at the kind of guilt that can be allayed by words or actions—the times when we *can* do something about our guilt by changing our behavior. The prisons have more than their share of people who feel no guilt. When guilt truly comes from the conscience, we need to take notice.

Guilt is healthy when we do something that's wrong or inappropriate or harmful. We feel guilty because we should feel guilty. Our guilt is teaching us a lesson that needs to be learned.

Josh, a man in his mid-thirties, called me up and said, "Dr. Gottlieb, I'm having a problem with my guilt and I want you to treat me."

During the first session, he told me his story. Up to a few months previously, he had been living with his parents and he had begun to feel guilty about it. During the past few years, he had started a small business, which had turned out to be very successful. He was rapidly becoming a wealthy man. "I felt as if I was living on the dole," he told me. "I had more money than my parents did, but I was still living in their house."

Josh came up with a creative idea. He would buy his own house. He told his parents that he planned to find a large house with a lot of extra room, so they could move in with him. That way, he decided, he would no longer feel he was "living on the dole." He would have no reason to feel guilty.

So he moved out. He bought a house and moved away from his parents. Meanwhile, his parents put their house on the market.

It took Josh's parents a couple of months to find a buyer, and in the interim, Josh began to enjoy living alone. When his parents finally called and said, "We have a buyer. We're ready to move in with you," he was dismayed.

He called them back and said, "You know what? I've been living alone for a couple of months, and I kind of like it. I think I'd like to continue living alone."

When this patient came to me, he hoped I would "cure" the guilt he felt about his behavior. He wanted me to make the guilt go away.

I couldn't, of course. Josh's guilt was completely healthy. It was "telling" him to change his behavior. He could talk about his anger, his hostility, and his dependency issues. But he also needed to make amends to his parents.

He realized that his guilt would not go away in therapy. His therapist could not "magically" make it vanish and make Josh feel better. But he could talk about where the guilt came from. Josh was aware that he had hurt his parents. He wanted to make amends. And he realized if he *could* make amends, it would help to allay the guilt.

Josh found his parents a condominium where they could live comfortably and independently. He took his parents to see the condo, and after they had approved it, he bought it for them. When they had settled in and it was apparent that they would be fine in their new home, Josh discovered that his guilt had dissipated.

When Frank Pittman talks about the guilt that "changes your behavior," he's addressing healthy guilt. We feel guilty when we've hurt somebody. We may be able to do something about it—we can decide to change our behavior. And we can make amends the best we can.

33

When We Feel Shame

∾

There's a wonderful "ziggy" cartoon in which poor Ziggy, almost cured of a guilt complex, is assailed with a dose of shame. And the assailant is his own psychiatrist.

In the first frame of the cartoon, Ziggy is lying on the psychiatrist's couch, and the psychiatrist is saying, "Ziggy, it has taken me longer to cure you of your guilt complex than any patient I've ever had."

In the second frame, the psychiatrist says to Ziggy, "You should be *ashamed* of yourself for making me work that hard!"

And so it's piled on—guilt for having such a terrible guilt complex and shame for feeling so guilty. Now who will cure Ziggy's "shame complex"?

Nora had been a secret drinker. In front of her husband, however, she had never had more than a few glasses of wine and always at appropriate times. Secretly she had been "doing shots, sneaking drinks behind his back," and hiding bottles of liquor.

Without telling her husband, Nora joined Alcoholics Anonymous. She eventually gave up drinking entirely. When her husband Milt noticed that she wasn't having her usual glasses of wine with dinner, Nora simply told him that she'd given it up. Milt accepted the change of pattern without congratulating her or giving her any special pat on the back.

Then Nora found that she wanted Milt to give her credit for what she'd done. And that meant he would have to know about the amount of secret drinking she had done before.

"I wanted him to say, 'You did a great job! It's really great you're not drinking anymore!' Nora said. Yet she was afraid of how he might react if she told him everything about her previous behavior.

"I knew what he'd say," she told me. "He'd say, 'Hey, if you can lie about something like that, I wonder what else you're lying about.' I knew he would interpret it as my lying to him—when, really, I wasn't lying. I was just so ashamed. I didn't want him to think he had a wife who was an alcoholic."

Shame is almost biological. It's part of our very core. Most of us, I'm sure, had a parent or teacher who told us, "You should be ashamed of yourself " when we misbehaved. And we were. Even if shame wasn't "taught" to us directly, we surely felt ashamed when people laughed at us, or got angry at us, or told us not to do something "ever again."

And what did we do with that shame?

I know what I did. My underachievement as a child was my shameful part. When I grew up and began my career, I became a workaholic. For the first ten years of my career, I held two full-time jobs. I strove to be perfect in everything I did. And my workaholism was related to shame: I was ashamed of the other part of myself—the mediocre part.

I think many addictions are connected to shame when we feel we need to hide our basic core. For example, if we're taught that we should be ashamed of our sexuality and shouldn't enjoy it, then what do we do with the sex drive that we're not "supposed" to have? We may overexpress it, becoming sex addicts and having numerous affairs. Or we may try to hide our shame, and the hiding can lead to impotence and other sexual problems. What we're really doing, in either case, is expressing indirectly our own shame about our sexuality.

A homosexual man called the show when my guest was Leo Madow, a training and supervising analyst at the Philadelphia Psychoanalytic Institute (and the author of *Guilt: How to Recognize and Cope with It*). The caller said, "I feel like I was taught shame and secrecy. As a child, being gay had to be kept a secret. And shame was certainly a big part of what I was taught to feel also. At this point I feel confused about guilt versus shame. My shame is not so much about a deed as about my identity— who I am. Society continues to tell me that I need to be ashamed of who I am and that I'm not okay as I am."

"The shame," said Dr. Madow, "is that you're not living up either to the standards of your parents or to your own standards. You're ashamed because you 'should' be heterosexual—that's the 'proper' thing to do—and anything else is below what you 'should' be. The guilt is the feeling that you're doing something wrong."

The caller described the "messages" he gets from his family as being a mixture of acceptance and disapproval: "The message I get is, 'Well, that's okay, we accept that—but it's not okay to talk about it.'"

Could he separate the voice that said, "*You* are not acceptable" from the voices that said, "*Your sexuality* is not acceptable," I wondered. I asked him to try: "I wonder what your parents are saying. Certainly your sexuality is not acceptable to them. It probably never will be. But I wonder whether they're really saying *you're* not acceptable. And it sounds like that's part of what you're experiencing from them. It might be helpful to clarify that."

Some weeks later, the caller wrote me a letter in which he described some of the conversation that he'd had with his parents. He had asked them whether they could still love him, even if they did not approve of his sexuality.

"Dad said he was repulsed by my sexuality," he wrote. "Mom said she still loved me, no matter what. For a while, Dad didn't say anything more, but finally he said I was still his son and he loved me, too."

In all likelihood, the young man's parents had never thought about making a distinction between their son and their son's sexuality. Once they were able to make that distinction, they were able to take their son back in. They might still feel ashamed, or repulsed, or embarrassed by his sexuality. But he could experience their love without experiencing the shame.

Shame is part of the human experience. Almost everyone has had the universal dream of being caught naked in a public place and feeling ashamed and frightened. That's a dream from the unconscious, and it arises because all of us feel shame about some of our behavior.

The trouble comes when we identify our *selves* as shameful and try to hide those parts that we're ashamed of. If I hide my vulnerability or I hide my underachievement, all that hiding can get in the way of letting me experience love from another person.

And shame distorts my experience of love, as, for instance, when I say, "Well, you say you love me—but if you really knew me, you would find me very unlovable." My experience of love is altered when I expect that the love will end when my true self is "exposed." And when I have that expectation, I may try to hide my shame in any way possible with "perfect" or "acceptable" behavior. Or I may test the other person ("How much does she *really* love me?") by behaving in a way that "proves" I'm not lovable after all.

Is there another way to deal with the shame?

You can deal with it simply by trusting yourself and talking about what you're ashamed of. The more we talk about our fears and our shame, the more human we will feel. We can be lovable as whole persons, not just as people who give an outstanding performance, overachieve, or behave well.

When Nora talked to her husband about giving up drinking, she was disappointed by his first reaction, which was, "Well, you weren't drinking that much anyway." Wanting more from him, she tried to show him that her achievement was greater than he realized. Perhaps if he knew how much she had been drinking in secret, she thought, he would give her more credit for giving it up! When she told him about "drinking behind his back" and hiding liquor from him, she still found his reaction unsatisfying. As she had anticipated and feared, he said, "If you could hide that from me, what else are you hiding?"

Nora tried to make her husband understand that her behavior was related to her drinking problem and that she had not tried to deceive him. Yet she continued to feel he didn't give her credit for coming as far as she had.

I asked her, "Does he know about your shame? Does he know that you feel so terribly ashamed of yourself that you couldn't admit it to him?" And I asked her to reinterpret her search for that pat on the back: "I would say that what you're hungry for is to be truly known by your husband. And what you want known is your core.

"Part of your core has to do with the shame. If you want to go even deeper, you can talk to your husband about what you're ashamed of. What you need to talk about is that very self that feels ashamed, and that's what you need to communicate to him—the real vulnerable parts."

In Nora's longing for approval was the hunger that we all have—the hunger to be known. And when shame is at the core of us, we can't be truly known unless we allow others to see that shame.

Nora was eventually able to talk to Milt about more than the drinking. She began to tell him some of what went on inside when she hid her behavior from him and when she drank by herself. That was the shame part. He never did congratulate her for overcoming her drinking problem. Yet when Nora was able to talk about what went on inside herself, she discovered that getting a pat on the back from Milt was not so important. She got something more. A shameful part of her became known—and she didn't lose her husband's love because of it. Nora began to feel as if all of her could be lovable, not just the behavior that she had "fixed," but also the part that made her feel ashamed.

34

Achievement: Is It Ever Enough?

༄

The world is full of people trying to be filet mignon
when deep down we know we're only meatballs.

—Tom Fogarty, family therapist

My caller was exact and articulate about what was bothering her:

> I feel a lot of shame for not living up to the image I por-
> tray. I'm a professional person. When I go to work each
> day, I try to do the best I can. But I can't help feeling that
> sooner or later someone's going to walk up to me and say,
> "Look, we know that you've done an adequate job, but
> you're not really good at it—and we'd like you to leave
> now!"

What she feared, she went on to say, was that someone would
find out she was a fake—that she wasn't really as smart, competent, and professional as she'd led everyone to believe. At work,
she was always worried that she "wasn't putting enough in." It
seemed to her that all her colleagues worked harder, applied
themselves more, and were better at keeping up with the literature and staying abreast of the latest advances in the field.

Looking back at how she had performed in school, she said, "Both my parents were successful. They expected a lot of me. When I got a 96, they always asked, 'Why didn't you get 100?'"

Was she angry at them, I wondered.

"Not really," she said. "They did well in school, so they just assumed I should do well in school. I don't know about the anger. I just have this fear that I'm going to be discovered. Usually late at night I lie in bed thinking, 'Tomorrow I'm going to do this and this, and I'm going to straighten out everything in my life and go on from there—and everything will be perfect.'"

"And you'll be in control again!"

"Right!"

"Okay, let me ask a ridiculous question. What's so bad about being *out* of control? What's the fear about? If I were to say, 'You're out of control,' what would you be afraid was going to happen?"

"I don't really know."

"Out-of-controlness feels real scary to most of us."

"It *is* scary."

"And it might help to know what you're scared of, rather than trying to control it."

"I enjoy my work," she said, "and it's something I wanted to do. But I'm afraid someone's going to take that away from me and say, 'Go find something else. You're a fake. You're not truly dedicated to what you're doing.'"

"I wonder whether there's a part of you that *wants* something else," I said.

"I don't know."

"I wonder what would happen if someone said to you, 'Go ahead—go find something else!'"

"I think it would be a relief."

"Exactly. There's a part of you that wants someone to come up and tap you on the shoulder. There's a part of you that's hollering, 'Pay attention to me!' From what you've said so far, I haven't been able to hear the voice real clearly. But I'll bet it hollers more loudly when you're in bed at night. It hollers more loudly to all of us when there are no other voices. Part of what that voice might be saying is, 'Maybe I want to play around with doing something else.' Or 'Maybe I'm angry.' Or 'Maybe I'm tired.' 'Maybe I'm resentful.' 'Maybe I'm all those things.' Or 'Maybe I'm just overcontrolled and I want to be out of control.'

"There are parts of you that you're just not listening to. And you're feeling guilty about those parts of you. But you just have to listen. You have to pay close attention to yourself. It's raging in there. It's calling out, *'Listen to me!'*"

One of the privileges of being host of a talk show is that one can occasionally turn preachy. And I knew why I had: I was describing voices that were familiar to me. I can still hear, very distinctly, all the teachers who said to me, "Dan, you have so much *potential!*"

That's supposed to sound like a compliment. But it didn't feel like one. It felt like an angry statement. It felt critical.

Who's to judge what *potential* each of us has? It's a very difficult thing.

The woman who called was still dismayed that she had had 96s when she could have had 100s. To me, 96s would have been academic nirvana. To her—still hearing her parents' voices—a 96 was four points lower than her "potential."

We see other people's potential through our own screen, especially if we're parents. We see our children's potential as we need to see it, rather than as it is. And we hear about our own potential from our parents. So it's difficult to judge for ourselves where our "potential" begins and ends. When a teacher said to me, "You have so much potential," I didn't know what to do next. What did it mean? What was that teacher trying to tell me?

The woman who called me had voices inside that were crying out, "You're overachieving!" Other voices were saying: "No, you're *underachieving!*" And beneath all that clamor was a voice saying, "Hear me! You're not *listening* to me! You're trying to achieve *around* me!" Why was she not hearing it?

Perhaps she was ashamed of the quality inside her. Perhaps there's a meatball there, when everyone has told her it's supposed to be filet mignon.

Maybe she learned from her family that 96 is meatball, or maybe it's meatball by her own definition. In either case, I have bad news for her. In all likelihood, 96 is all she's capable of achieving without harming herself or harming the quality of her life.

I have a wonderful fantasy—that she could stand up in front of her parents, her colleagues, and herself, and announce, "What I am, everybody, is a 96 kind of person, and I've made my peace with that." And if she could do that, then she wouldn't be an overachiever *or* an underachiever anymore. She could be happy with what she *was* achieving.

Understanding the meaning of achievement is part of our tropism—our personal journey in the discovery of the adult self. Our parents may have seen us as professional, academic, athletic, or artistic achievers, and those "measures" of achievement are part of the archaic self. But as we grow into our adult selves, ideally achievement will become something that depends on the tropism in our lives.

That's what I was hoping this caller could "achieve"—to make her peace with being a 96 kind of person, so she could enjoy her life more.

So many of the patients who come into my office criticize themselves for not living up to their own potential. My question for them is, "What if you *are* living up to your potential? What if you're already there? What would the ramifications be?"

Almost without exception, people say, "It would be a relief. I'd be more at peace with my life."

Is there *any* achievement that's ever "enough"?

To know that for ourselves, we may have to reconsider what we are calling achievements. If we are really meatballs, if we're *never* going to be filet mignon, what is it that meatballs can achieve?

I treated a man who had been recently diagnosed as having a liver disorder, and he was facing the imminence of his own death. The medical prognosis was that he would probably have less than ten years to live. In therapy he talked about fears of his death, and I asked him to tell me what he would like to do with the rest of his life.

"I'd like to achieve my potential at work," he said.

I pursued it. "Why do you want to achieve your potential?"

He talked about a possible promotion and salary increase. It turned out he was especially concerned about paying off the balance due on his charge accounts and credit cards.

I wanted to know why that was a priority. "What difference will it make if you don't pay off your credit cards?" I asked him. "You'll be dead! The vendors will be stuck with the bill!"

He laughed.

And then I said, "Come on. Assume you're terminally ill. You've got ten years. What do you want to do?"

Then he thought about his grandchildren. He talked about his wife. He talked about how he wanted to enjoy his life more. But he couldn't figure out a way to work less and still maintain his lifestyle.

By the end of the session, he was toying with the idea of selling his house and moving into an apartment. He was beginning to figure out ways to get some of the enjoyment he wanted in his life.

We don't need a therapist to help us become aware of what we need. The voices that come from inside will tell us. We begin to discover symptoms—our unhappiness, our anxiety, our insomnia. Or our fatigue, our anger, and our resentment. And we overachieve to try to hide those symptoms.

Achievements are like bandages. They cover things over, but they don't heal. We need to heal from the inside, and that's a process that takes a long time. We don't get more from life by adding more things to the surface. It's been said a thousand times: what we really long for is not more cars, more money, more degrees, more houses. It's something deeper and more personal—closer to security, love, and finding meaning in one's life.

There's something coming from our hearts that needs to be listened to. And we have to listen very carefully, rather than trying to achieve ourselves out of it.

35

How Do We Live with Our Secret Selves?

ॐ

Most of us attach labels to the kinds of behavior that we believe are bad or wrong. Sadistic behavior falls into this category, as do harmful or destructive outbursts. Murderous actions are bad. So are certain expressions of sexuality. So are reckless actions that endanger people.

When we see crimes acted out on TV or reported in the newspaper, we deplore the behavior of the sadist, the criminal, the sexual deviant, the sociopath. And most if not all the time, when we detect those impulses in ourselves, we recognize them as unacceptable. We don't act out those impulses in a violent, abusive, or deviant form.

Yet those "unacceptable" impulses are still parts of ourselves. Carl Jung, one of the founders of modern psychoanalysis, talked about those parts becoming our "shadows." The shadows are our secret selves, and the way we learn about them is generally through dreams, and sometimes through fantasies. Occasionally they get acted out.

If we repress these impulses, we may wind up working for a person or marrying a person who acts out some part of our selves that we are reluctant to express. If we're intensely competitive but afraid to show it, we may choose to be close to a business colleague who is fiercely competitive. If we can't deal with our own anger, we may marry an angry person and deal with their anger rather than our own.

Our shadows are the secret parts of us that we can't tolerate. Most of us try to get rid of those parts—or pretend they're not there. They follow us around, nonetheless. We can't run away from them.

Apart from the shadows that we can characterize as bad or wrong, there are others that we may hide even though they seem less explosive or dangerous. For a man, femininity may be the shadow; for a woman, masculinity. Underachievement may be a shadow for one person; mediocrity, for another.

These kinds of secret selves may seem less fearsome than the more demonic-looking shadows that are composed of murderous, sadistic, or cruel impulses. Yet the less-fearsome shadows may be just as intolerable to us. We can't tolerate the "opposite" side of ourselves, and often those shadows become a source of shame.

One of the families that I treated was that of a very prominent Philadelphia lawyer who was one of the head partners in a thriving law firm. His wife was a successful management consultant who had continued her profession while raising two children. Both were extremely active in civic organizations. Their children were a seventeen-year-old son who was taking all-honors courses in private school and a fourteen-year-old daughter who was also an outstanding student. The daughter was anorexic.

In our first session, the father told me that he was suffering from an ulcer and hypertension. He talked about his frustrations at work and at home. At his firm, he said, he felt he was accomplishing about half of what he was capable of doing. He planned to reorganize his office soon in order to improve everyone's efficiency and become more effective.

He complained about "the way things are at home. I know if I turn my back for a minute, things won't get done," he said. "I can't handle every little thing," he went on, giving his wife a meaningful look, "but I'm not getting the cooperation I need."

I asked his wife and his daughter to talk about what life was like for them. They painted a picture of a well-organized but rigid family system. With work and planned events, all of them were on tight schedules.

After the other family members had had a chance to speak, I turned back to the father and said: "You have obviously accomplished a great deal. You have a good job. You have a very nice family. What if this is all there is to your life?"

He shook his head. "I won't accept that. I know what my goals are—and I have a lot to accomplish."

"And what if you won't accomplish all those things?" I asked. "What if you've lived up to your potential already?"

For a moment he looked stunned. Then he became furious with me. His wife and children seemed surprised by his reaction.

At the end of the session, neither the father nor the mother suggested making another appointment. For several weeks afterward, I didn't hear from the family. Then I got a call from the father, saying, "I'd like to talk to you."

He stayed in therapy for about a year and a half. During that time he realized what had made him angry: it was my suggestion that perhaps he had already lived up to his potential. As he began to accept that, he had to deal with sadness, grief, and mourning.

With the loss came a tremendous sense of relief. He began to enjoy his life.

What the father began to accept was his own mediocrity. That was the shadow that he had lived with, the shadow that he couldn't tolerate. His secret self was the part of him that was mediocre and always would be. He would never "live up to his potential" because there was nothing to "live up to." He was already there. He wasn't perfect; he was just adequate.

The whole family came to see me several times. I encouraged the children to talk about what life was like for them. They recognized that both their parents were perfectionistic. The children were raised with the expectation that they, too, would become achievers.

Eventually, the father was better able to live with the qualities in himself that were, by his own standards, just mediocre. As that happened, the other members of the family had permission to be less demanding of themselves. His daughter had been trapped by the perfectionism; she wanted to have the perfect body. As the dynamics of the family changed and she became less demanding of herself, her anorexia improved.

As we have seen, often our secret selves, our shadows, do not look like demons. The "shadow" is just our opposite; it's what we would like to hide. For a successful professional person who has excelled in his or her field, the shadow could be mediocrity. For someone who is a helpful, eager caregiver, the shadow might be anger or hostility. A person who appears to be independent and self-sufficient is likely to be pursued by the shadow of underachievement.

The more we acknowledge our shadows and learn to live with them, the less shameful they will be, and the more we will be able to talk about them and feel known. And those shadows will be less likely to pop up in our working lives and in our marriages.

My own shadow is my hatred. The first time I was in therapy the therapist began the session by asking me, "Why are you in therapy?"

"Because nobody hates me," I told him.

It was almost a joke, but a joke with a nod toward the truth. My complaint was that I was just "a nice guy." I felt I wasn't eliciting enough passion—either love *or* hatred.

I wasn't really saying I wanted people to hate me. Rather, I wanted to deal with my own hatred—the hatred I couldn't tolerate. My hatred is my shadow. There's a part of me that hates—just as there's a part of me that loves. And I was so afraid of my shadow that I couldn't be passionate. That was my secret self. I couldn't elicit passion in other people because I was afraid that my shadow-hatred would be seen, my secret self would emerge.

With that experience in therapy, I started to grow and mature within. And I became more comfortable acknowledging the rage inside me that was part of my shadow.

At one point, I attended a production of *Peter Pan* at my daughter's school. It was the first time I'd been exposed to the *Peter Pan* story as an adult, and I found myself reacting a bit perversely to the opening scene. In that scene, Peter Pan comes into Wendy's room looking for his shadow. I felt like yelling at him, "Peter, *you got rid of it!* Some of us spend our whole lives trying to do that. *Run like hell!*"

None of us ever does get rid of his shadow. Wishing it away doesn't help. Perhaps the better course would be to lift that shadow, gently, get to know it, and dance with it for a while. And when we put it back down, to accept that it will always follow us. That way it can become less fearful to us—and certainly less shameful. Since we can't walk away from our secret self, we might as well live with it and deal with it, acknowledging it as a permanent guest in our lives.

36

When Are We Trying to Change Our Selves?

❧

God grant me the serenity to
accept the things I cannot change,
The courage to change the things I can,
And the wisdom to know the difference.

—"The Serenity Prayer," Alcoholics Anonymous

In our quick-fix society, when we hear a voice that's distressing we want to silence it immediately. So when we "hear" back pain, we want to take a pill for it. What we haven't been trained to do is simply sit back and listen to the voice and understand the part of ourselves that's trying to talk.

We could take a lesson from the Buddhists who just sit and listen. We have to listen to our souls. Real change comes of doing so rather than from lessons in "How to Be a Better Parent" or "How to Be a Better Worker." The change in our soul grows out of the process of just listening and being able to hear ourselves. And then from making peace with the person we're hearing and the parts we're hearing, rather than trying to change those parts and manipulate our feelings.

—∿—

Christy was a woman who said she felt "stuck in the past."

"I want to go *forward,*" she began, the morning she called the show. "There's a part of me that wants to take that leap—to take that risk. I know that intellectually, okay? But I don't know it emotionally."

Christy's marriage had broken up about a year before. She was still suffering, and she wanted to escape the pain. But she felt stuck with it.

My guest on the show was Dr. Alex McCarty, a Jungian psychologist. He talked with the caller about her use of the word *leap* to describe how she wanted to break away from her past and "go forward."

"Leaping scares me," said Dr. McCarty. "I don't like leaping. I mean, kangaroos do that. If I'm going to consider change, it's going to be with 'fear and trembling' rather than 'leaping.' Maybe you can find that part within you that *trembles* with change."

I suggested to Christy that she had already, that morning, taken one step toward change when she picked up the phone.

"I guess I'd like an *instant* change, and that's where the word 'leap' comes from," she replied.

I noted that we all have that unrealistic wish for instant change. What steps, I asked, had she already taken in the process of change? Were there any? Was life any different for her now than it had been a year ago?

"There have been little steps."

"How? Where?"

"Number one, I've survived. Number two, I'm not nearly as devastated as I might have been a year ago."

"Good. I love it. Go on!"

"I take pride in my work. I take pride in my home."

"Anything else?"

"I've taken some risks. I've been invited to parties, and I've gone all by myself. That was real hard."

"I know."

"So . . . here I am."

"Well," I said, "so much for leaping, huh?"

"But it still hurts."

"Yeah. The suffering hurts and the losses hurt. They sure do. The kind of mourning you're going through doesn't end quickly."

"I'd like to put it in a microwave," said Christy, "and make it better."

"Yeah," I said, "I know."

Was she disappointed that I didn't have the microwave? In a certain respect, a call-in program is another creation of a microwave society; many people who pick up the phone to call want to have something "fixed." Although that doesn't happen, they are likely to wind up feeling heard and acknowledged and feeling the richer for it. And perhaps that's something we're missing in our efforts to have things fixed. Maybe, ultimately, what we're looking for is to be acknowledged, to be heard by ourselves, our loved ones, our culture, and our family, rather than to have things fixed.

On the same show I had a call from a woman who worked in the career-guidance department of a large corporation. She talked about the "energy" that she felt was part of her, and she described the way people frequently encouraged her to be more assertive and to express herself more emphatically.

"People are always saying, 'You need to accept your authority. You need to let that energy be *out* there.' I think, 'That sounds great and I can feel the energy there.' And yet when I actually try to take that step—to go out into the world—it's like I don't quite exactly know where to go."

And how was she doing right now?

She said she had been in bed for two weeks with back pain. During that time, she said, she had been telling herself she needed to make drastic changes in her life.

"I tried 'imaging,'" she said. "You know, focusing on what changes I need to make. But I feel physically stuck."

I asked her to tell me more about the people who kept telling her what she needed to do. "They're good people," she said. "They're helpful, and they feel I have a lot to share. I feel that way myself. They tell me there's a need for my energy."

"They're people who love you—telling you what you need to do."

"People who love me, yes," she said.

I told her about the loving, helpful people who kept reminding me of my potential when I was growing up—and how, for me, the words that *sounded* loving didn't *feel* loving. The way I heard it, those people were telling me that I was not adequate or acceptable the way I was right then. They were informing me that I needed to change something in order to be acceptable to them.

"I don't think you need to do anything," I said. "I think your back is giving you a message. Maybe you need to lie down and not do a damn thing for a while. Maybe you need to just be."

"Well, that's where I am."

"And that's where the growth is. Trust your body and trust your soul. They're taking you in a direction where you need to go. Okay? Just listen carefully."

I was about to add something else when the caller said, "Thank you!" and hung up. And what I was about to add was an apology for not giving her an Rx for her back pain. I was sure she had called for concrete advice—and I hadn't given it to her. Yet her sincere "thank you" indicated that she had heard all she wanted: I'd given her permission just to lie in bed. And that's what she had needed to hear.

I don't think we can change our core—what we're made of. We can't change the parts of ourselves that are shameful or embarrassing. We can't exorcise our anger, our mediocrity, our sadism, or our masochism.

What my caller was saying initially was, "Change me! Help me ignore my back!" But if I'd helped her do that, it would have made her symptoms worse.

We're just not trained very well at listening. So when our anger feels out of control, instead of trying to control it, let's listen. What are we angry about? Are we *feeling* attacked? Are we *being* attacked? Well, what's attacking us?

Or when we're feeling depressed—what's that depression all about? Maybe there are losses that need to be grieved. Instead of trying to exorcise the depression, let's find out what those losses are.

We can't have parts of our personality exorcised. We can't "microwave" our pain, as Christy wished, and make it better. What we can do is integrate our parts and make peace with them and be less ashamed of them. We can listen to those parts when they speak.

We may hide from our psychic needs, but ultimately they will find a voice and they will speak to us. How? They might speak to us through hypertension, through back pain, through our children's misbehaving, or our marriage's breaking up. And ultimately, do what we may, we will hear from all the different parts of our character structure that need to make their voices heard.

37

When We Think About Death

∽

"The last time I went to my parents' house for the holidays," a friend told me, "I stayed in my old bedroom. My mother had redecorated the room. There were family pictures hanging on the wall, and some old family photographs on the dresser. There was a picture of my grandfather and his brothers when they were young men. A picture of Dad before he went off to war, and of Mom and Dad when they were married. Pictures of my sister and me when we were kids. And there were some photographs of my own kids, taken the year before.

"Lying there in bed, just before I fell asleep, I looked around at those pictures and I felt something like vertigo. For a moment I didn't know whether I was still the kid in the photograph with my sister, and my life was starting out, or whether I'd been through all the passages of life and I was approaching the end. It was a 'timeless moment.' And I realized what was timeless about it—that I didn't know where I was in my own life. I was scared that my life might be almost over. I felt I hadn't lived enough for it to be ending. Or maybe I was at some kind of new beginning— and then I tried to remember what life had once looked like, when it all stretched ahead of me, with all its possibilities. I felt my own death approaching—but I didn't know how near it was, or how far away."

None of us can live twenty-four hours a day with an awareness of our own death. We know we're going to die, and yet most of us go along with the childlike notion that we're going to live forever. Even when we realize intellectually we're going to die, most of the time we don't believe it.

Linn Vanderhof is a family therapist who served as chaplain in the hospice program at Paoli Hospital in Pennsylvania. When I interviewed her on my program, Linn talked about the stages of grief and mourning that many people go through at the death of someone who's close to them. The year before, Linn had had a life-threatening accident when she took a twenty-foot fall from a balcony. She spoke of the fears that the accident evoked: "We tend to expect that our lives will continue as they are. We're assaulted emotionally and physically when life changes—and particularly when it changes in such a traumatic way. After my fall, I was fearful that something more would happen to me. No matter how competent or how successful I would try to become, there were things beyond my control."

And as I listened to her, the word that came to me was *betrayed*. When I had my accident, I felt betrayed. I can't say by what. Perhaps I felt betrayed by the world—or by my set of assumptions about the world. That sense of betrayal left me angry and afraid.

The unconscious experiences death as a murder. So when we feel death approaching or when a life-threatening accident happens, we rail at the injustice. We're out looking for the murderer. If someone we love has died, we may be angry at that person for "murdering" himself or herself. Or we're angry at the doctor. Or we look at ourselves and wonder what more we could have done. However we target our rage, we're looking for the murderer so we can demand justice. But what we're really railing at are the facts of life.

Age does not necessarily "prepare" us to make peace with death. I once asked an eighty-three-year-old woman who was a patient of mine to tell me her feelings about dying. She said she wasn't ready to die, and when I asked, "Why not?", she was delightfully honest in her reply.

"I'm not ready to give up control," she said.

Every death is an injustice. Losing your child is an injustice. Losing your parent or your mate is an injustice. Despite the reality that we can know intellectually—the reality that we're going to die—our own death strikes us as a terrible injustice. We experience death with each loss throughout our lives, beginning in infancy. And I don't think we ever make peace with it. The feelings of betrayal, of murder, of being wronged, are always there.

Sartre said, "Live with death on your shoulder."

I don't know whether anyone can completely do that. I struggle with it. Yet, I feel death is never very far away. The friend who went home for the holidays and slept in his old bedroom has experienced a loss. Part of his life was gone—but how much? Half of it? Most of it? For a moment he lost track of the signals that we use to tell us where we think we stand in the passage from birth to death. He knew that his life was not just beginning, and he had no reason to believe that it would soon be over. Yet he was acutely aware of his own life's passing—and of the necessity of living in the moment.

I struggle with my own death quite a bit, and I work hard to be prepared to die. I know it could happen at any moment. And I take it as my responsibility to do what I need to do to prepare for death.

What is that responsibility? To minimize the stress on myself and enjoy whatever time I have left. It could be six months, six years, or forty years. I feel as if I am terminally ill, and I don't know how rapidly the terminal illness is progressing. I'm not aware of it all the time. If I were, I think I would be depressed. But death is there for me. As a result, I'm able to enjoy life more. And I am less afraid of those who are dying.

One week, I visited an AIDS workshop at an AIDS drop-in center. The purpose of my visit was to tape an open discussion that would later be aired on *Voices in the Family*. Before going to the drop-in center, I was very frightened about doing a program with people who were dying or terminally ill. By the end of the program, I was exhilarated. These weren't people who were dealing with death. They were dealing with life despite their deaths. They were living in fuller ways than most people I know.

I like to say that's what I'm able to do—that I'm able to enjoy life more because I'm not afraid of dying. I appreciate the days that are relatively stress-free. I'm aware of my life; I'm in tune with it. I don't assume I have tomorrow.

I think all of us have the capacity to live in the moment, no matter how near or far away our own death appears. Sharon, a patient, talked about her mother, who had recently died. Sharon said her mother had always been somewhat depressed, and her depression had become almost unremitting as her death approached. I asked Sharon to tell me about the last time she remembered her mother's laughing.

She thought for a moment and said, "You know, Mama's brother came to visit just a few days before she died. The two of them were talking about their memories, and they both started laughing. And the more they remembered, the more they laughed."

And I thought: How delightful! Isn't that a wonderful statement about the human spirit? Here was a woman who knew she was in the last moments of her life, and she was able to laugh anyway.

And I think that's our responsibility—to enjoy our lives the best we can, up to the last moment, rather than to resist.

38

Making Peace with Our Selves

∾

The caller was a woman in her thirties, the mother of three children. She broke out laughing several times during our conversation. She wasn't depressed. She wasn't angry. She just wanted to make very sure her kids wouldn't grow up to be as bad as she had been when she was a teenager.

Bad?

Well, she said, she'd been allowed to "run wild" when she was seventeen and eighteen. Looking back, she blamed a lot of her bad behavior on her school. She now thought the environment had been much too unrestricted. She had been allowed to "get away with stuff" in that school—and now she wanted to make sure her own three kids didn't follow the same path.

"The bad girl that was there at eighteen is still inside you," I reminded her, "but she's not a bad girl. And I think the more you try to ignore her or squish her or put her out of your mind, the more you're going to be afraid of her."

"She was bad," the caller exclaimed—and started laughing.

"You're laughing!"

"I know!"

"You're giving us both a message."

"I know," she said, "but I look at my kids and I say to myself, 'Hey, I don't want them to go through the misery that I brought upon myself!'"

"If you can make peace with yourself and with that other part of yourself, your children are much less likely to go through the 'misery.' They'll have a happier, more comfortable mother."

"I see," she said. She paused. "I see," she repeated. "Yes, I think I'm beginning to see something. Okay!"

And I had an image of her looking in a mirror at herself and literally "seeing something" that she hadn't seen before. What she saw was a "bad girl," but perhaps it was a "girl" she could live with instead of trying to exorcise.

Years ago, there was a time when I was angry at my life, angry at my disability, and angry at myself. I was feeling sorry for myself. As I was brushing my hair one morning, I stopped and looked at myself in the mirror. And I flashed back to my adolescence.

Like so many teenagers, I used to spend hours just looking in the mirror. Now, many years later, I recognized the eyes that I had seen in the mirror years before. These were truly the same eyes. *There* was the same kid who used to play Wiffle ball! And as I looked at those eyes, I liked that kid. That moment, when I saw the same kid inside who had been there all along, was a very powerful moment in my life. I saw the person inside that I needed to make peace with—the person inside who needed love.

We really owe it to ourselves to find that person who is hungry, hurting, or sad—the person who feels ashamed and vulnerable. And we need to be loving and gentle with that person.

We can't say, "I will love myself if I achieve more . . . if I complete this course . . . if I can be less angry." No contingencies!

That's not the kind of love we needed from our parents, and it's not the kind of love we need from ourselves.

We have to provide ourselves with unconditional love and affection. And in order to do that, we have to give up on a lot of wishes, fantasies, and dreams about what we could be, should be, or ought to be. We need to make peace with ourselves as we are *right now*.

During the writing of this book, as I've told you, I suffered a tragedy in my marriage, with a separation that ended in divorce. At one point, there were a couple of days when I was feeling increasingly anxious and panicky and angry at myself. Knowing myself—and knowing how the human species tends to work—I was aware that there was something underneath it that I wasn't allowing myself to feel. And I knew it had to do with my grief over the loss of my marriage and the loss of the family I had known.

I drove to Fairmount Park, and for about an hour I sat overlooking the Schuylkill River. And I forced myself to think about my early marriage. I thought about the excitement and joy of the wedding and the two kids—Sandy and me—who became newlyweds. I remembered an early apartment that we had lived in and the birth of our first child. I wouldn't allow myself to think of anything else except, perhaps, the ducks on the river. I tried very hard not to think of the bad times, the pain, the losses. I just remembered the joys.

And as I thought of my past life that was dying, I wept by myself at the river. I felt terribly, terribly sad, and at the same time, all of the anxiety and rage began to dissipate. I felt depressed. I felt a tremendous sense of loss. But I felt real.

A family pulled up next to me—a beautiful family in a battered car—and everyone got out to look at the river. The mother and father appeared to be in their late thirties. They had three children: a son who was about seventeen, a daughter who was about fourteen, and another daughter who looked about four or five.

For a while, they all sat together by the river. Then the younger daughter ran off to play, and the teenage boy followed to look after her. The father bantered with his older daughter, and she got angry and stormed away. They distracted me from grieving over my marriage. And I looked at this family and I thought about my family and what I'd lost. I just sat and looked, smiling, enjoying, and appreciating every one of them.

Ultimately, we are alone.

Despite the fact that we are products of our families and we carry our families inside us, we have to give up what doesn't work. We have to give up any unrealistic hope we carry. We have to grieve our losses—to enable us to find a new self. Once we've given up unrealistic hope, we can go back to a new family. We can begin to appreciate the members of that family for what they are and jettison what they are not.

When I was thirteen years old, just before my bar mitzvah, I happened to spend some time in a room by myself for a couple of hours. It wasn't planned that way. It was just happenstance. The rest of the family was getting ready, and I was left to myself. It was a time of reflection. And that was a profound experience for me. I remember thinking, "Where is the *me* in all this? What does it all mean?"

Then the bar mitzvah began and I was among family and friends—and no one knew that I had changed in those hours alone.

Some thirty years later, I was alone again, and again I had to find the *me* in all this. It was the same self and yet changed. The thirteen-year-old boy was still there, preparing for his bar mitzvah, but he was gone, too. And all the guests and friends and relatives had come and gone many times through the years.

I was watching the river and I was also part of the river, the same self moved by the currents and sitting by the shore. And I felt serene, to be moving and yet the same, to be part of the river yet separate from its flow—to be making my peace with my self, the day, and the family despite all the losses.

Conclusion: A Note on Healing

Not long ago, I received a letter from a woman who had attended an "open show" in the WHYY studio. When I have an open show, members of the audience are invited to ask questions or make comments which will later be aired on Voices in the Family. Though this woman did not have an opportunity to speak at the forum, she later wrote me:

> It's easy to understand that you are a psychologist and a therapist. What is rarer is that you are a healer. . . .
>
> I wanted to step up to the microphone and ask you about this because it seemed to me that you yourself had become the focal point of something like a healing process on the part of your audience. It felt as though the people who had come to hear you were doing more than that: we were really *pulling* for you. . . .
>
> Driving up a steep hill the other day, I found myself "pulling" for a biker struggling up the grade against a cold wind. I thought, "In primitive societies, what I am doing is regarded as natural. I wonder how many other

drivers are 'pulling' with this biker in the same way. Does the biker feel our pull?"

I want to add something to what this woman has to say about healing. First of all, I think she was right: the people in that audience were *pulling* for me, and that pulling had something to do with the healing process that was taking place.

I can't say whether the biker could "feel" the pull of the woman who was writing this letter—I'm inclined to think not. But the woman's act of pulling for the biker is healing for her. Moreover, the audience's pulling for me is healing for them. It's an act of generosity. By instinct, almost, they connect with someone who is vulnerable and pull for that person. And because I can trust that they are pulling for me, that makes the vulnerability feel safe for me and for them.

People who saw me in the hospital after my accident—when I showed my vulnerability and talked about it—were able to love me in a way that felt safe and gratifying to them. The more vulnerable I was, the safer it was to love me.

And we all know that love is healing.

I think love is healing regardless of the direction it goes in. My dog would often come up to me when I was needy—when I was hurt or depressed or worried. He'd be wagging his tail. Well, what happened then? I would rub his stomach. I'd nurture him. The question, though, was who was nurturing whom? Did the dog *want* me to feel better? It was not important to know that. He was blind to my needs, yet in his presence I felt nurtured.

So the *direction* of nurturing is not important. People do not have to make coffee for me in order to be nurturing. The healing process is not necessarily *doing something* for loved ones who are in need. It's just the experience of loving—or, as the letter referred to, the experience of "pulling for" someone.

Other things are healing, as well.

When I taught introductory classes in psychotherapy, I would tell my students that their first and primary responsibility was to create an environment of safety for the families they work with, or the patients they work with. The world feels unsafe to most of us, and I think relationships feel unsafe. Even our families feel unsafe. But *an experience of safety* is healing.

When we arrive in a truly safe, protective environment, we're free to grow and to develop and to touch different parts of our emotional selves. I think part of the way we create safety is through *respect*—respecting the integrity, respecting the dignity, respecting the inner psychic strength of people. I respect the ability of people to manage their own lives and I respect the human spirit.

The first time I went into a physical therapy gym, I saw people whose bodies were far more broken than mine, people who had fewer resources and fewer loved ones. They had less insurance than I did—which means they had fewer financial resources. Yet I watched them laugh and I watched them not take themselves too seriously. I watched them enjoy what they had.

There's nothing special about me, and nothing special about them. But I think the human spirit is special.

Because the human spirit rarely is challenged, we rarely know how special it is. I consider it my job, as a therapist and a healer, to create a safe environment, to have true respect for the dignity and strength of the human spirit, and to allow that spirit to grow.

I am pulling. But I am not pulling for change. I am pulling to heal the individual or to heal the family that embodies that spirit.

What else does a healer do?

I think he removes whatever is blocking the human spirit from healing itself or from being healed. What might be blocking it? All of the topics I have discussed in this book could be blocking the spirit—depression, addiction, unexpressed rage or resentment. The spirit could be blocked by never having had the experience of finding safety. Or the spirit could be blocked because it has never been valued.

I don't heal a person by "lifting" these blocks away. I can only create a healing environment. People heal themselves.

So I don't try to change people. I think it's disrespectful to say, "I want to change you." And I think that urging people to change themselves makes for an unsafe environment. If someone comes into my office and says, "I need to change," that person is saying, "There is a part of me that is defective." And if I agree with that person and say, "Okay, I will help you change," what I'm actually implying is, "Yes, there's a part of you that's broken."

What I choose to say is, "No, I don't accept that premise. There's not a part of you that's bad. There's a part of you *that you can't tolerate*. And I'll help you tolerate it. But I won't help you exorcise it." And so the parts that people want to throw away are integrated instead.

In my position of respecting the human psyche, I respect the ability to integrate all parts of the human psyche. I also respect the fact that another person's dark side is not all that dark—no darker than mine or anybody else's.

The words *integrate* and *integrity* come from the same root. If we've got parts of us that are "cut off," "cut away," "not integrated"—parts that we want to "change" or "fix"—then we lack integrity. And when our *psyches* lack integrity, our *spirits* lack integrity.

In many ways, the role of "healer" is much like the role of "teacher."

I am reminded of a teaching story that was written by Milton Erickson, a world-renowned psychiatrist who was stricken with polio in his teens and confined to a wheelchair in later life.

As a boy growing up in a rural area, Erickson came home one day to find a stray horse waiting by his doorstep. Neither he nor his friends knew who owned the horse. He climbed onto the horse and started up the road. The horse wandered along at its own pace. Every now and then it would stray off the road, and Erickson would bring him back. But he did not try to lead the horse in any particular direction.

Eventually, horse and rider came to a farmhouse, and the horse turned in.

A farmer appeared at the door. "That's my horse."

"Yes, I know," Erickson replied.

The farmer asked, "How did you know it was my horse?"

And Erickson said, "I didn't. All I did was keep him on the road, and he eventually got to where he needed to go."

Healing is part of the process that takes place in a safe environment with someone we're very intimate with and trusting with—with someone who keeps us on the road but doesn't tell us where to turn.

—⁓—

Healing is also coming to grips with certain undeniable truths and making peace with them. Truths like, "Life is hard" or "At a certain level, we're all lonely." Truths like, "Nobody's parents ever gave him exactly what he wants and needs. There's always unfinished business." And truths like, "We can never find serenity or peace until we give something up."

I think if we make these discoveries in a safe environment with someone we trust—with someone we know who respects us at the very deepest levels—that's healing.

And I think only wounded people can be healers. I obviously am wounded. I think most of us are wounded, but many of us don't acknowledge those wounds. The wounds I feel in my soul are comparable to the wounds someone else might feel who has said good-bye to a dying spouse, who has grown up with an alcoholic parent, who has lost a child, or who is a product of a divorce.

I acknowledge my wounds; I can't deny them; I don't have the luxury. Those of us who don't deny our wounds can be healers. And all of us come to know what's healing for ourselves.

I know that what's healing for me is when I feel somebody's trust, when I feel a person's love and respect. When people say to me, "Thank you for who you are—for being there," that's healing. When someone touches my shoulder or holds my hand—that's healing. In my experience, the *being there* is more healing than any words.

In my teaching, I tell therapists that healing in therapy is about sixty percent *who you are* and forty percent *what you do*. The language is simply a vehicle to communicate affection or to create an environment of safety. The words themselves are not all that meaningful. If someone were to hold my hand, that action alone might be more meaningful than the most astute verbal analysis of what's happening to me or what I'm feeling. I know what heals because I can *feel* healing. And I can feel the warmth of healing because I also feel the pain of my wounds.

I think all people in the helping professions are somewhere on the continuum of healer. No one becomes the ultimate healer—that would be some divine spirit. But we can move on that continuum.

After my accident, I moved on the continuum. I moved because I lost power. I lost strength. In many respects, I lost resources. So, now, all I can do is sit and watch and be. The only thing I have to offer people now is what I have inside me.

I used to value what I had *outside* me. I used to think my self-worth was in how much I could do: "Can I cook a meal?" "Can I pour somebody coffee?" I believed that my actions determined my worth.

Now I can't do any of those things.

But I have come to trust that *just being* is valuable, not just for me but for others.

Acknowledgments

I remain grateful to the many people who helped me write this book, which was first published by Dutton in 1991. I am thankful for the valuable advice and guidance I received from my late close friend Darrell Sifford, a trusted adviser throughout the writing process. I also feel a good deal of gratitude toward my agent, Jane Dystel, for supporting this book and guiding it to its rightful place. I especially thank Jane for introducing me to Ed Claflin. When we first met, Ed was simply a pen for my voice. But over the many months it took us to write this book, we got to know one another. I felt Ed could truly hear my heart (and I hope I heard his), and I gained a trusted friend.

Our fine editor at Dutton was Alexia Dorszynski, who provided much-needed advice, encouragement, and support.

Ed Claflin, Jane Dystel, and my wonderful editor Patty Gift at Sterling Publishing have been instrumental in bringing this new edition into print.